# $\mathcal{E}$ASY

# $\mathcal{W}$EDDING $\mathcal{P}$LANNER

## With FREE
## Wedding Planning Software!

## Concise and Easy to Read

By
Elizabeth & Alex Lluch
Professional Wedding Consultants

Written by Elizabeth & Alex Lluch
Professional Wedding Consultants

**Published by Wedding Solutions Publishing, Inc.**
© Copyright 2000

**Reviewed and Approved by:**
Wilda Hyer,
California State Coordinator for the Association of Bridal Consultants; Owner of *Events Plus,* Ceres, California;
and Gayle Labenow,
New York Metro Coordinator for the Association of Bridal Consultants; Owner of *You Are Cordially Invited,* Babylon, New York.

**Front Cover Photograph & Back Cover 1st, 3rd & 4th Provided By:**
Karen French, *Karen French Photography*
8351 Elmcrest
Huntington Beach, CA   92646
(800) 734-6219
www.karenfrenchphotography.com

**Back Cover 2nd Photograph Provided By:**
Jon Barber, *Barber Photography*
34085 Pacific Coast Highway #117
Dana Point, CA   92629
(949) 493-5840
www.barberphotography.com

**Cover Design by:**
Amy Allen Graphics, San Diego, CA

Printed in China

ISBN 1-887169-15-6

*T*HE WEDDING OF

_____

&

_____

*W*HO WILL BE MARRIED ON

_____

*A*T

_____

# *D*EDICATED TO:

All brides and grooms.
May their wedding day be the
happiest day of their life!

# $\mathscr{C}$ONTENTS

# *I*NTRODUCTION

*D*ear Bride and Groom:

Congratulations on your engagement!  You must be very excited for having found that special person to share the rest of your life with.    And you must be looking forward to what will be the happiest day of your life -- your wedding!  Planning your wedding can be fun and exciting.  But it can also be very stressful.  That is why Wedding Solutions Publishing, Inc., a professional wedding planning company, created *Easy Wedding Planner with FREE Software*.

*Easy Wedding Planner* begins with a very detailed wedding planning checklist containing everything you need to do or consider when planning your wedding and the best time frame in which to accomplish each activity.  Each item in the checklist is followed by the page number(s) where that item is explained within the book.

The checklist is followed by a comprehensive and detailed budget analysis, listing all the expenses that are typically  incurred in a wedding as well as the percentage of the total budget that is typically spent in each category.  Each expense item in the budget is followed by the page number(s) where that item is explained within the book.  This makes it very easy to find detailed information on each item.

The budget analysis is followed by a detailed description of each item in the budget including:   Options, Things To Consider, Questions To Ask, Things To Beware Of, Tips To Save Money, and Price Ranges.   Our clients find this format to be both informative and easy to use, and we know you will too!

Next is a short chapter on Wedding Traditions, explaining the symbolic meaning and historical purpose of some of the more common wedding traditions, and a list of "Do's" and "Don'ts" when planning your wedding.

Lastly, we have included a list of responsibilities for each member of your wedding party as well as the traditional formations for the ceremony, processional, recessional and receiving line for both Jewish and Christian weddings. We have also included traditional seating arrangements at the reception.

The *Easy Wedding Planning Software for Windows* gives you the ability to completely organize and manage all of your necessary wedding plans. It was designed with two things in mind: first, to enable you to store and quickly retrieve all the many details pertaining to your wedding (expenses, things to do, guests, etc); and second, to be as easy to use and as intuitive as possible. You will find this software to be a great addition to *Easy Wedding Planner*. For your reference, you will find a User's Manual on page 199.

We are confident that you will enjoy planning your wedding with the help of *Easy Wedding Planner* and *Easy Wedding Planning Software for Windows*. So come join the many couples who have used our books to plan a stress-free wedding. Also, if you know other options, things to consider, tips to save money, or anything else that you would like to see included in this book, please write to us at: Wedding Solutions Publishing, Inc.; 6347 Caminito Tenedor; San Diego, CA 92120. We will include your ideas or suggestions in our next printing. We listen to brides and grooms like you -- that is why *Easy Wedding Planner* has become the best wedding planning book available!

Sincerely,

Elizabeth H. Lluch

# WEDDING PLANNING CHECKLIST

This Wedding Planning Checklist itemizes everything you need to do or consider when planning your wedding, and the best time frame in which to accomplish each activity.

As you can see, many of the items are followed by the page number(s) where those items are explained in more detail within the book. This will help you find the information you need, when you need it.

This checklist assumes that you have nine months or more to plan your wedding. If your wedding is in less than nine months, just start at the beginning of the list and try to catch up as quickly as you can!

Use the boxes to the left of the items to check-off the activities as you accomplish them. This will enable you to see your progress and help you determine what has been done and what still needs to be done.

This comprehensive Wedding Planning Checklist is also available as a large poster (9.5" x 23") which can be mounted on any surface such as a wall, refrigerator, door or mirror. This attractive and convenient poster allows you to see your wedding planning progress at a glance.

This checklist is available through Wedding Solutions Publishing, Inc. for $5.95.  As a special offer to our readers, you may order it free of charge.  To receive this poster, simply fill out the Order Form on page 259.

## *Nine* Months and Earlier

| | Page |
|---|---|
| Announce your engagement. | |
| Select a date for your wedding. | |
| Hire a professional wedding consultant. | 157 |
| Determine the type of wedding you want: location, formality, time of day, number of guests, etc. | 33 |
| Determine budget and how expenses will be shared. | 21 |
| Develop a record-keeping system for payments made. | 195 |
| Consolidate all guest lists: bride's, groom's, bride's family, groom's family, and organize as follows: <br> 1) those who must be invited <br> 2) those who should be invited <br> 3) those who would be nice to invite | |
| Decide if you want to include children among guests. | |
| Select and reserve ceremony site. | 33 |
| Select and reserve your officiant. | 35 |
| Select and reserve reception site. | 91 |
| Select and order your bridal gown and headpiece. | 39 |
| Determine your color scheme. | |

| *N*ine Months and Earlier (Cont.) | *P*age |
|---|---|
| Buy a calendar and note all important activities: showers, luncheons, parties, get-togethers, etc. | 151 |
| If ceremony or reception is at home, arrange for home or garden improvements as needed. | |
| Order passport, visa or birth certificate, if needed for your honeymoon or marriage license. | |
| Select and book photographer. | 51 |
| Select maid of honor, best man, bridesmaids and ushers (approx. one usher per 50 guests). | 173 |

## *S*ix to Nine Months Before Wedding

| | |
|---|---|
| Select flower girl and ring bearer. | 182 |
| Give the *Wedding Party Responsibility Cards* to your wedding party. | 173 |
| Reserve wedding night bridal suite. | |
| Select attendants' dresses, shoes and accessories. | |
| Select flower girl's dress, shoes and accessories. | |
| Select and book caterer, if needed. | 95 |
| Select and book ceremony musicians. | 107 |
| Select and book reception musicians or DJ. | 109 |
| Schedule fittings and delivery dates for yourself, attendants, flower girl and ring bearer. | |
| Select and book videographer. | 61 |
| Select and book florist. | 119 |

## *Four* to Six Months Before Wedding

| | Page |
|---|---|
| Start shopping for each other's wedding gifts. | 147 |
| Reserve rental items needed for ceremony & reception. | 141 |
| Finalize guest list. | |
| Select and order wedding invitations, announcements and other stationery such as thank-you notes, wedding programs, and seating cards. | 67 |
| Address invitations or hire a calligrapher. | 85 |
| Set date, time and location for your rehearsal dinner. | 151 |
| Arrange accommodations for out-of- town guests. | |
| Start planning your honeymoon. | |
| Select and book all miscellaneous services, i.e. gift attendant, valet parking, etc. | 105 |
| Register for gifts. | |
| Purchase shoes & accessories. | 44 |
| Begin to break-in your shoes. | 45 |

## *Two* to Four Months Before Wedding

| | |
|---|---|
| Select bakery and order wedding cake. | 113 |
| Order party favors. | 102 |
| Select and order room decorations. | 137 |

| *Two* to Four Months Before Wedding (Cont) | *Page* |
|---|---|
| Purchase honeymoon attire & luggage. | |
| Select and book transportation for wedding day. | 139 |
| Check blood test and marriage license requirements. | 154 |
| Shop for wedding rings and engrave them. | |
| Consider having your teeth cleaned or bleached. | |
| Consider writing a will and/or prenuptial agreement. | 155 |
| Plan activities for your out-of-town guests both before and after the wedding. | |
| Purchase gifts for wedding attendants. | 148, 149 |

## *Six* to Eight Weeks Before Wedding

| | |
|---|---|
| Mail invitations. Include accommodation choices and a map to assist guests in finding the ceremony and reception sites. | 67, 78 |
| Maintain a record of RSVPs and all gifts received. Send thank-you notes upon receipt of gifts. | 82 |
| Determine hair style and makeup. Have hairdresser work with your headpiece. | 46 |
| Schedule to have your hair, makeup and nails done the day of the wedding. | 47 |
| Finalize shopping for wedding day accessories such as toasting glasses, ring pillow, guest book, etc. | 37, 117 |

| Six to Eight Weeks Before Wedding (Cont.) | Page |
|---|---|
| Set up an area or a table in your home to display gifts as you receive them. | |
| Check with your local newspapers for wedding announcement requirements. | 153 |
| Have your formal wedding portrait taken. | 59 |
| Send wedding announcement & photograph to your local newspapers. | 153 |
| Change name & address on drivers license, social security card, insurance policies, subscriptions, bank accounts, memberships, etc. | |
| Select and reserve wedding attire for groom, ushers, father of the bride and ring bearer. | 47 |
| Select a guest book attendant. Decide where and when to have guests sign in. | 36 |
| Mail invitations to rehearsal dinner. | 151 |
| Get blood test and health certificate. | 154 |
| Obtain marriage license. | 154 |
| Plan a luncheon or dinner with your bridesmaids. Give them their gifts at that time or at the rehearsal dinner. | 148, 151 |
| Find "something old, something new, something borrowed, something blue, and a six pence (or shiny penny) for your shoe." | 162 |
| Finalize your menu, beverage and alcohol order with your caterer. | 95, 97 |

| *Two* to Six Weeks Before Wedding | *Page* |
|---|---|
| Confirm ceremony details with your officiant. | 35 |
| Arrange final fitting of bridesmaids' dresses. | |
| Have final fitting of your gown and headpiece. | 42, 43 |
| Finalize rehearsal dinner plans;  arrange seating and write names on place cards, if desired. | 151 |
| Make final floral selections. | 119 |
| Make a detailed schedule for your wedding party. | |
| Make a detailed schedule for your service providers. | |
| Confirm details with all service providers, including attire.  Give them a copy of your wedding schedule. | |
| Start packing for your honeymoon. | |
| Finalize addressing and stamping announcements. | 85 |
| Decide if you want to form a receiving line.  If so, determine when and where to form the line. | 165 |
| Contact guests who haven't responded. | |
| Pick up rings and check for fit. | |
| Meet with photographer and confirm special photos you want taken. | 52 |
| Meet with videographer and confirm special events or people you want videotaped. | 61 |
| Meet with musicians and confirm music to be played during special events such as first dance. | 107 |

| *T*wo to Six Weeks Before Wedding (Cont.) | *P*age |
|---|---|
| Continue writing thank-you notes as gifts arrive. | 82 |
| Remind bridesmaids and ushers of when and where to pick up their wedding attire. | |
| Purchase the lipstick, nail polish and any other accessories you want your bridesmaids to wear. | 149 |
| Determine ceremony seating for special guests. Give a list to the ushers. | |
| Plan reception room layout and seating with your reception site manager or caterer.  Write names on place cards for arranged seating. | 77 |

## *T*he Last Week

| | |
|---|---|
| Pick up wedding attire and make sure everything fits. | |
| Do final guest count and notify your caterer or reception site manager. | |
| Gather everything you will need for the rehearsal and wedding day as listed in the *Wedding Party Responsibility Cards*. | 191 |
| Arrange for someone to drive the getaway car. | 175 |
| Review the schedule of events and last minute arrangements with your service providers. | |
| Confirm all honeymoon reservations and accommodations.  Pick up tickets and travelers checks. | |
| Finish packing your suitcases for the honeymoon. | |

| The Last Week (Cont.) | Page |
|---|---|
| Familiarize yourself with guests' names. It will help during the receiving line and reception. | |
| Have the Post Office hold your mail while you are away on your honeymoon. | |

## The Rehearsal Day

| | Page |
|---|---|
| Review list of things to bring to the rehearsal as listed in the *Wedding Party Responsibility Cards.* | 191 |
| Give your bridesmaids the lipstick, nail polish and accessories you want them to wear for the wedding. | 148 |
| Give best man the officiant's fee and any other checks for service providers. Instruct him to deliver these checks the day of the wedding. | |
| Arrange for someone to bring accessories such as flower basket, ring pillow, guest book & pen, toasting glasses, cake cutting knife and napkins to the ceremony and reception. | |
| Arrange for someone to mail announcements the day after the wedding. | 81 |
| Arrange for someone to return rental items such as tuxedos, slip and cake pillars after the wedding. | 141 |
| Provide each member of your wedding party with a detailed schedule of events for the wedding day. | |
| Review ceremony seating with ushers. | |

| *The Wedding Day* | *Page* |
|---|---|
| Review list of things to bring to the ceremony as listed in the *Wedding Party Responsibility Cards*. | 192 |
| Give the groom's ring to the maid of honor. Give the bride's ring to the best man. | 174, 175 |
| Simply follow your detailed schedule of events. | |
| Relax and enjoy your wedding! | |

# Personal Notes

_____

_____

_____

_____

_____

_____

_____

_____

_____

_____

_____

_____

_____

_____

_____

_____

_____

_____

_____

_____

_____

_____

# $\mathscr{B}$UDGET $\mathscr{A}$NALYSIS

This comprehensive Budget Analysis has been designed to provide you with all the expenses that can be incurred in any size wedding, including such hidden costs as taxes, gratuities and other "items" that can easily add up to thousands of dollars in a wedding. After you have completed this budget, you will have a much better idea of what your wedding will cost. You can then prioritize and allocate your expenses accordingly.

This budget is divided into fifteen categories: Ceremony, Wedding Attire, Photography, Videography, Stationery, Reception, Music, Bakery, Flowers, Decorations, Transportation, Rental Items, Gifts, Parties, and Miscellaneous.

At the beginning of each category is the percentage of your wedding budget that is typically spent in that category, based on national averages. Multiply your intended wedding budget by this percentage and write that amount in the "typical" space provided.

To determine the total cost of your wedding, estimate the amount of money you will spend on each item in the budget analysis and write that amount in the "Budget" column after each item. Next to each expense item is the page number where you can find detailed information about that item. Items printed in italics are traditionally paid for by the groom or his family.

Add all the "Budget" amounts within each category and write the total amount in the "Budget Subtotal" space at the end of each category. Then add all the "Subtotal" figures to come up with your final wedding budget. The "Actual" column is for you to input your actual expenses as you purchase items or hire your service providers. Writing down the actual expenses will help you stay within your budget.

For example, if your total wedding budget is $10,000, then write this amount at the top of page 23. To figure your typical ceremony expenses, multiply $10,000 x .05 (5%) = $500.00. Write this amount on the "Typical" line under the "Ceremony" category to serve as a guide for all your ceremony expenses.

If you find, after adding up all your "Budget Subtotals," that the total amount is more than what you had in mind to spend, simply decide which items are more important to you and adjust your expenses accordingly.

The section immediately following the Budget Analysis provides a full explanation of each item in the budget, including a full description of the item or service, options available for that item or service, things to consider when purchasing or hiring that item or service, questions to ask in order to make the best buying decision, things to beware of, tips to save money, and a price range for each item or service, based on national averages.

# *B*udget *A*nalysis

**Your Wedding Budget**   $_____

**CEREMONY**

(Typical = 5% of Budget)  $_____

|  | BUDGET | ACTUAL | PAGE |
|---|---|---|---|
| Ceremony Site Fee | $_____ | $_____ | 33 |
| *Officiant's Fee* | $_____ | $_____ | 35 |
| *Officiant's Gratuity* | $_____ | $_____ | 36 |
| Guest Book, Pen, Penholder | $_____ | $_____ | 36 |
| Ring Bearer Pillow | $_____ | $_____ | 37 |
| Flower Girl Basket | $_____ | $_____ | 37 |
| Subtotal 1 | $_____ | $_____ |  |

**WEDDING ATTIRE**

(Typical = 10% of Budget)   $_____

|  | BUDGET | ACTUAL | PAGE |
|---|---|---|---|
| Bridal Gown | $_____ | $_____ | 39 |
| Alterations | $_____ | $_____ | 42 |
| Headpiece & Veil | $_____ | $_____ | 43 |

| WEDDING ATTIRE (CONT.) | BUDGET | ACTUAL | PAGE |
|---|---|---|---|
| Gloves | $ | $ | 44 |
| Jewelry | $ | $ | 44 |
| Stockings | $ | $ | 45 |
| Garter | $ | $ | 45 |
| Shoes | $ | $ | 46 |
| Hairdresser | $ | $ | 46 |
| Makeup Artist | $ | $ | 46 |
| Manicure/Pedicure | $ | $ | 47 |
| *Groom's Formal Wear* | $ | $ | 47 |
| | | | |
| Subtotal 2 | $ | $ | |

**PHOTOGRAPHY**

(Typical = 9% of Budget) $_____

| | BUDGET | ACTUAL | PAGE |
|---|---|---|---|
| Bride & Groom's Album | $ | $ | 51 |
| Parents' Album | $ | $ | 56 |
| Extra Prints | $ | $ | 56 |
| Proofs/Previews | $ | $ | 57 |
| Negatives | $ | $ | 57 |
| Engagement Photo | $ | $ | 59 |
| Formal Bridal Portrait | $ | $ | 59 |
| | | | |
| Subtotal 3 | $ | $ | |

## VIDEOGRAPHY

(Typical = 5% of Budget)  $_____

|  | BUDGET | ACTUAL | PAGE |
|---|---|---|---|
| Main Video | $\_\_\_\_\_ | $\_\_\_\_\_ | 61 |
| Titles | $\_\_\_\_\_ | $\_\_\_\_\_ | 64 |
| Extra Hours | $\_\_\_\_\_ | $\_\_\_\_\_ | 64 |
| Photo Montage | $\_\_\_\_\_ | $\_\_\_\_\_ | 65 |
| Extra Copies | $\_\_\_\_\_ | $\_\_\_\_\_ | 65 |
| Subtotal 4 | $\_\_\_\_\_ | $\_\_\_\_\_ | |

## STATIONERY

(Typical = 4% of Budget)  $_____

|  | BUDGET | ACTUAL | PAGE |
|---|---|---|---|
| Invitations | $\_\_\_\_\_ | $\_\_\_\_\_ | 67 |
| Response Cards | $\_\_\_\_\_ | $\_\_\_\_\_ | 74 |
| Reception Cards | $\_\_\_\_\_ | $\_\_\_\_\_ | 75 |
| Ceremony Cards | $\_\_\_\_\_ | $\_\_\_\_\_ | 76 |
| Pew Cards | $\_\_\_\_\_ | $\_\_\_\_\_ | 77 |
| Seating/Place Cards | $\_\_\_\_\_ | $\_\_\_\_\_ | 77 |
| Rain Cards | $\_\_\_\_\_ | $\_\_\_\_\_ | 78 |
| Maps | $\_\_\_\_\_ | $\_\_\_\_\_ | 78 |
| Ceremony Programs | $\_\_\_\_\_ | $\_\_\_\_\_ | 79 |
| Announcements | $\_\_\_\_\_ | $\_\_\_\_\_ | 81 |
| Thank-You Notes | $\_\_\_\_\_ | $\_\_\_\_\_ | 82 |

| STATIONARY (CONT.) | BUDGET | ACTUAL | PAGE |
|---|---|---|---|
| Stamps | $_____ | $_____ | 82 |
| Calligraphy | $_____ | $_____ | 83 |
| Napkins and Matchbooks | $_____ | $_____ | 83 |
| | | | |
| Subtotal 5 | $_____ | $_____ | |

**RECEPTION**

(Typical = 35% of Budget)    $_____

| | BUDGET | ACTUAL | PAGE |
|---|---|---|---|
| Reception Site Fee | $_____ | $_____ | 91 |
| Hors D'oeuvres | $_____ | $_____ | 94 |
| Main Meal/Caterer | $_____ | $_____ | 95 |
| Liquor/ Beverages | $_____ | $_____ | 97 |
| Bartending/Bar Set-up | $_____ | $_____ | 100 |
| Corkage Fee | $_____ | $_____ | 100 |
| Fee to Pour Coffee | $_____ | $_____ | 100 |
| Service Providers' Meals | $_____ | $_____ | 101 |
| Gratuity | $_____ | $_____ | 102 |
| Party Favors | $_____ | $_____ | 102 |
| Disposable Cameras | $_____ | $_____ | 103 |
| Rose Petals/Rice | $_____ | $_____ | 104 |
| Gift Attendant | $_____ | $_____ | 105 |
| Parking Fee/Valet | $_____ | $_____ | 105 |
| | | | |
| Subtotal 6 | $_____ | $_____ | |

**MUSIC**

(Typical = 5% of Budget)  $\underline{\hspace{3cm}}$

|  | BUDGET | ACTUAL | PAGE |
|---|---|---|---|
| Ceremony Music | $\underline{\hspace{2cm}}$ | $\underline{\hspace{2cm}}$ | 107 |
| Reception Music | $\underline{\hspace{2cm}}$ | $\underline{\hspace{2cm}}$ | 109 |
| Subtotal 7 | $\underline{\hspace{2cm}}$ | $\underline{\hspace{2cm}}$ | |

**BAKERY**

(Typical = 2% of Budget)  $\underline{\hspace{3cm}}$

|  | BUDGET | ACTUAL | PAGE |
|---|---|---|---|
| Wedding Cake | $\underline{\hspace{2cm}}$ | $\underline{\hspace{2cm}}$ | 113 |
| *Groom's Cake* | $\underline{\hspace{2cm}}$ | $\underline{\hspace{2cm}}$ | 115 |
| Cake Delivery & Set-up Fee | $\underline{\hspace{2cm}}$ | $\underline{\hspace{2cm}}$ | 115 |
| Cake-Cutting Fee | $\underline{\hspace{2cm}}$ | $\underline{\hspace{2cm}}$ | 116 |
| Cake Top | $\underline{\hspace{2cm}}$ | $\underline{\hspace{2cm}}$ | 116 |
| Cake Knife/Toast Glasses | $\underline{\hspace{2cm}}$ | $\underline{\hspace{2cm}}$ | 117 |
| Subtotal 8 | $\underline{\hspace{2cm}}$ | $\underline{\hspace{2cm}}$ | |

**FLOWERS**

(Typical = 6% of Budget)  $\underline{\hspace{3cm}}$

| FLOWERS (CONT.) | BUDGET | ACTUAL | PAGE |
|---|---|---|---|
| **BOUQUETS** | | | |
| *Bride's* | $_____ | $_____ | 119 |
| Tossing | $_____ | $_____ | 123 |
| Maid of Honor's | $_____ | $_____ | 123 |
| Bridesmaids' | $_____ | $_____ | 124 |
| **FLORAL HAIRPIECE** | | | |
| Maid of Honor/ Bridesmaids' | $_____ | $_____ | 124 |
| Flower Girl's | $_____ | $_____ | 125 |
| **CORSAGES** | | | |
| *Bride's Going Away* | $_____ | $_____ | 125 |
| *Other Family Members'* | $_____ | $_____ | 126 |
| **BOUTONNIERES** | | | |
| *Groom's* | $_____ | $_____ | 127 |
| *Ushers and Other Family's* | $_____ | $_____ | 128 |
| **CEREMONY FLOWERS** | | | |
| Main Altar | $_____ | $_____ | 129 |
| Alter Candelabra | $_____ | $_____ | 130 |
| Aisle Pews | $_____ | $_____ | 130 |

| RECEPTION FLOWERS | BUDGET | ACTUAL | PAGE |
|---|---|---|---|
| Reception Site | $_____ | $_____ | 131 |
| Head Table | $_____ | $_____ | 131 |
| Guest Tables | $_____ | $_____ | 132 |
| Buffet Table | $_____ | $_____ | 133 |
| Punch Table | $_____ | $_____ | 133 |
| Cake Table | $_____ | $_____ | 133 |
| Cake | $_____ | $_____ | 134 |
| Cake Knife | $_____ | $_____ | 134 |
| Toasting Glasses | $_____ | $_____ | 135 |
| Floral Delivery & Setup | $_____ | $_____ | 135 |
| | | | |
| Subtotal 9 | $_____ | $_____ | |

**DECORATIONS**

(Typical = 3% of Budget)  $_____

| | BUDGET | ACTUAL | PAGE |
|---|---|---|---|
| Table Centerpieces | $_____ | $_____ | 138 |
| Balloons | $_____ | $_____ | 138 |
| | | | |
| Subtotal 10 | $_____ | $_____ | |

**TRANSPORTATION**

(Typical = 2% of Budget)  $_____

| TRANSPORTATION (CONT) | BUDGET | ACTUAL | PAGE |
|---|---|---|---|
| Transportation | $_____ | $_____ | 139 |
| | | | |
| Subtotal 11 | $_____ | $_____ | |

**RENTAL ITEMS**

(Typical = 3% of Budget)  $_____

| | BUDGET | ACTUAL | PAGE |
|---|---|---|---|
| Bridal Slip | $_____ | $_____ | 141 |
| Ceremony Accessories | $_____ | $_____ | 141 |
| Tent/Canopy | $_____ | $_____ | 143 |
| Dance Floor | $_____ | $_____ | 144 |
| Tables/Chairs | $_____ | $_____ | 144 |
| Linen/Tableware | $_____ | $_____ | 145 |
| Heaters | $_____ | $_____ | 146 |
| Lanterns | $_____ | $_____ | 146 |
| Other | $_____ | $_____ | 146 |
| | | | |
| Subtotal 12 | $_____ | $_____ | |

**GIFTS**

(Typical = 3% of Budget)  $_____

| | BUDGET | ACTUAL | PAGE |
|---|---|---|---|
| *Bride's Gift* | $_____ | $_____ | 147 |
| Groom's Gift | $_____ | $_____ | 147 |

| GIFTS (CONT.) | BUDGET | ACTUAL | PAGE |
|---|---|---|---|
| Bridesmaids' Gifts | $_____ | $_____ | 148 |
| *Ushers' Gifts* | $_____ | $_____ | 149 |
| | | | |
| Subtotal 13 | $_____ | $_____ | |

**PARTIES**
(Typical = 4% of Budget)  $_____

| | BUDGET | ACTUAL | PAGE |
|---|---|---|---|
| Bridesmaids' Luncheon | $_____ | $_____ | 151 |
| *Rehearsal Dinner* | $_____ | $_____ | 151 |
| | | | |
| Subtotal 14 | $_____ | $_____ | |

**MISCELLANEOUS**
(Typical = 4% of Budget)  $_____

| | BUDGET | ACTUAL | PAGE |
|---|---|---|---|
| Newspaper Announcements | $_____ | $_____ | 153 |
| *Marriage License* | $_____ | $_____ | 154 |
| *Prenuptial Agreement* | $_____ | $_____ | 155 |
| Bridal Gown Preservation | $_____ | $_____ | 156 |
| Bouquet Preservation | $_____ | $_____ | 156 |
| Wedding Consultant | $_____ | $_____ | 157 |
| Wedding Planning Software | $_____ | $_____ | 159 |

| MISCELLANEOUS (CONT.) | BUDGET | ACTUAL | PAGE |
|---|---|---|---|
| Taxes | $_____ | $_____ | 159 |
| Subtotal 15 | $_____ | $_____ | |
| TOTAL (Add "Budget" & "Actual" Subtotals 1-15") | $_____ | $_____ | |

# *C*EREMONY

## CEREMONY SITE FEE

The ceremony site fee is the fee to rent a facility for your wedding. In churches, cathedrals, chapels, temples, or synagogues, this fee may include the organist, wedding coordinator, custodian, changing rooms for the bridal party, and miscellaneous items such as kneeling cushions, aisle runner, and candelabra. Be sure to ask what the site fee includes prior to booking a facility. Throughout this book, the word church will be used to refer to the site where the ceremony will take place.

**Options:**   Churches, cathedrals, chapels, temples, synagogues, private homes, gardens, hotels, clubs, halls, parks, museums, yachts, wineries, beaches, and hot air balloons.

**Things To Consider:**   Your selection of a ceremony site will be influenced by the formality of your wedding, the season of the year, the number of guests expected and your religious affiliation. Make sure you ask about restrictions or guidelines regarding photography, videography, music, decorations, candles, and rice or rose petal-tossing. Consider issues such as proximity of the ceremony site to the reception site, parking availability, handicapped accessibility, and time constraints.

**Questions To Ask:**   Make sure you ask all the following questions before selecting a ceremony site:

- What is the name & phone number of my contact person?
- What dates & times are available?
- How much time will be allotted for my ceremony?
- Do vows need to be approved?
- What is the ceremony site fee?
- What is the payment policy?
- What is the cancellation policy?
- Does the facility have liability insurance?
- What are the minimum & maximum number of guests allowed?
- What is the denomination, if any, of the facility?
- What restrictions are there with regards to denomination?
- Is an officiant available?  At what cost?
- Are outside officiants allowed?
- Are any musical instruments available for our use?
- If so, what is the fee?
- Are there are any music restrictions?
- Are there are any photography restrictions?
- Are there are any videography restrictions?
- Are there are any restrictions for rice or rose petal-tossing?
- Are candlelight ceremonies allowed?
- What floral decorations are available/allowed?
- When is my rehearsal to be scheduled?
- Is a dressing room available?
- Is there handicap accessibility and parking?
- How many parking spaces are available for my family & wedding party? Where are they located?
- How many parking spaces are available for my guests?
- What rental items are necessary?

**Tips To Save Money:**  Have your ceremony at the same facility as your reception to save a second rental fee.  Set a realistic guest list and stick to it.  Hire an experienced wedding consultant.  At a church or temple, ask if there is another wedding that day and share the cost of floral decorations with that bride.  Membership in a

church, temple or club can reduce rental fees.   At a garden
wedding, have guests stand and omit the cost of renting chairs.

**Price Range:**  $100 - $800

## OFFICIANT'S FEE

The officiant's fee is the fee paid to whomever performs your
wedding ceremony.

**Options:**   Priest, Clergyman, Minister, Pastor, Chaplain, Rabbi,
Judge, or Justice of the Peace.

Discuss with your officiant the readings you would like
incorporated into your ceremony.  Some popular readings are:

| | |
|---|---|
| Beatitudes | Corinthians 13:1-13 |
| Ecclesiastes 3:1-9 | Ephesians 3:14-19; 5:1-2 |
| Genesis 1:26-28 | Genesis 2:4-9, 15-24 |
| Hosea 2:19-21 | Isaiah 61:10I |
| John 4:7-16 | John 15:9-12, 17:22-24 |
| Mark 10:6-9 | Proverbs 31:10-31 |
| Romans 12:1-2, 9-18 | Ruth 1:16-17 |
| Song of Solomon | Tobit 8:56-58 |

**Things To Consider:**    Some officiants may not accept a fee,
depending on your relationship with him/her.  If a fee is refused,
send a donation to the officiant's church or synagogue.

**Tips To Save Money:**  Consider the officiant's fee when selecting
your officiant and your ceremony site.

**Price Range:**  $50 - $500

## OFFICIANT'S GRATUITY

The officiant's gratuity is a discretionary amount of money given to the officiant for performing your wedding.

**Things To Consider:**   This amount should depend on your relationship with the officiant and the amount of time s/he has spent with you prior to the ceremony.  The groom puts this fee in a sealed envelope and gives it to his best man or wedding consultant, who gives it to the officiant either before or immediately after the ceremony.

**Price Range:**  $25 - $250

## GUEST BOOK / PEN / PENHOLDER

The guest book is a formal register where your guests sign-in as they arrive at the ceremony or reception.  It serves as a memento of who attended your wedding.  This book is often placed outside the ceremony or reception site, along with an elegant pen and penholder.  A guest book attendant is responsible for inviting all guests to sign-in.  A younger sibling or close friend who is not part of the wedding party may be well-suited for this position.

**Options:**   There are many styles of guest books, pens and penholders to choose from.  Some books have space for your guests to write a short note to the bride and groom.

**Things To Consider:**  Make sure you have more than one pen in case one runs out of ink.  If you are planning a large ceremony (over 300 guests), consider having more than one book and pen so that your guests don't have to wait in line to sign-in.

**Price Range:**  $10 -$75

## RING BEARER PILLOW

The ring bearer, usually a boy between the ages of four and eight, carries the bride and groom's rings or mock rings on a pillow. He follows the maid of honor and precedes the flower girl or bride in the processional.

**Options:**  These pillows come in many styles and colors. You can find them at most gift shops and bridal boutiques.

**Things To Consider:**  If the ring bearer is very young (less than 7 years), place mock rings on the pillow in place of the real rings to prevent losing them.  If mock rings are used, instruct your ring bearer to put the pillow upside down during the recessional so your guests don't see the mock rings.

**Tips To Save Money:**  Make your own ring bearer pillow by taking a small white pillow and attaching a pretty ribbon to it to hold the rings.

**Price Range:**  $5 - $35

## FLOWER GIRL BASKET

The flower girl, usually between the ages of four and eight, carries a basket filled with flowers, rose or paper rose petals to strew as she walks down the aisle.  She follows the ring bearer or maid of honor and precedes the bride during the processional.

**Options:**  Flower girl baskets come in many styles and colors. You can find them at most florists, gift shops, and bridal boutiques.

**Things To Consider:**   Discuss any restrictions regarding rose petal, flower, or paper-tossing with your ceremony site.   Select a basket which complements your guest book and ring bearer pillow. If the flower girl is very young (less than 7 years), consider giving her a small bouquet instead of a flower basket.

**Tips To Save Money:**   Ask your florist if you can borrow a basket and attach a pretty white bow to it.

**Price Range:**   $5 - $35

# *W*EDDING *A*TTIRE

## BRIDAL GOWN

Bridal gowns come in a wide variety of styles, materials, colors, lengths and prices. You should order your gown at least four to six months before your wedding if your gown has to be ordered and then fitted.

**Options:** Different gown styles can help create a shorter, taller, heavier, or thinner look. Here are some tips:

**A short, heavy figure:** To look taller and slimmer, avoid knit fabrics. Use the princess or A-line style. Chiffon is the best fabric choice because it produces a floating effect and camouflages weight.

**A short, thin figure:** A shirtwaist or natural waist style with bouffant skirt will produce a taller, more rounded figure. Chiffon, velvet, lace and Schiffli net are probably the best fabric choices.

**A tall, heavy figure:** Princess or A-line are the best styles for slimming the figure; satin, chiffon and lace fabrics are recommended.

**A tall, thin figure:** Tiers or flounces will help reduce the impression of height. A shirtwaist or natural waist style with a full skirt are ideal choices. Satin and lace are the best fabrics.

The guidelines below will help you select the most appropriate gown for your wedding:

**Informal wedding:**
Street-length gown or suit
Corsage or small bouquet
No veil or train

**Semi-formal wedding:**
Floor-length gown
Chapel train
Finger-tip veil
Small bouquet

**Formal daytime wedding:**
Floor-length gown
Chapel or sweep train
Fingertip veil or hat
Gloves
Medium-sized bouquet

**Formal evening wedding:**
Same as formal daytime
except longer veil

**Very formal wedding:**
Floor-length gown
Cathedral train
Full-length veil
Elaborate headpiece
Long sleeves or long arm-covering gloves
Cascading bouquet

**Things To Consider:**   In selecting your bridal gown, keep in mind the time of year and formality of your wedding.  It is a good idea to look at bridal magazines to compare the various styles and colors. If you see a gown you like, call boutiques in your area to see if they carry that line.  Always try on the gown before ordering it.

When ordering a gown, make sure you order the correct size. If you are between sizes, order the larger one. You can always have your gown tailored down to fit, but it is not always possible to have it enlarged. Don't forget to ask when your gown will arrive, and be sure to get this in writing. The gown should arrive at least six weeks before the wedding so you can have it tailored and select the appropriate accessories to complement it.

**Questions To Ask:** The following questions may help you select a source for your bridal gown:

- What are your hours of operation?
- Are appointments needed?
- Do you offer any discounts or give-aways?
- What major bridal gown lines do you carry?
- Do you carry outfits for the mother of the bride?
- Do you carry bridesmaids gowns?
- Do you carry outfits for the flower girl and ring bearer?
- Do you rent tuxedos?
- What is the cost of the desired bridal gown?
- What is the cost of the desired headpiece?
- Do you offer in-house alterations? If so, what are your fees?
- Do you carry bridal shoes? What is their price range?
- Do you dye shoes to match outfits?
- Do you rent bridal slips? If so, what is the rental fee?
- What is the estimated date of delivery for my gown?
- What is your payment policy?
- What is your cancellation policy?

**Beware:** Some bridal boutiques have the practice of ordering gowns a size larger than needed. This requires more alterations which may mean extra charges. Ask for all alteration pricing in advance. Tailoring is a great source of income for boutiques. Also, gowns often fail to arrive on time, creating unnecessary stress for you. Have the store manager state, in writing, when the gown will arrive. And be sure to check the reputation of the boutique before buying.

**Tips To Save Money:** Consider renting a gown or buying one secondhand. Renting a gown usually costs about forty to sixty percent of its retail price. Consider this practical option if you are not planning to preserve the gown. The disadvantage of renting, however, is that your options are more limited. Also, a rented gown usually does not fit as well as a custom tailored gown.

Ask about discontinued styles and gowns. Watch for clearances and sales, or buy your gown "off the rack."

Restore or refurbish a family heirloom gown. If you have a friend, sister, or other family member who is planning a wedding, consider purchasing a gown that you could both wear. Change the veil and headpiece to personalize it.

**Price Range:** $300 - 3,000

## ALTERATIONS

Alterations may be necessary in order to make your gown fit perfectly and conform smoothly to your body.

**Things To Consider:** Alterations usually require several fittings. Allow four to six weeks for alterations to be completed. However, do not alter your gown months before the wedding. Your weight may fluctuate during the final weeks of planning and the gown might not fit properly. Alterations are usually not included in the cost of the gown.

You may also want to consider making some modifications to your gown such as shortening or lengthening the train, customizing the sleeves, beading and so forth.  Ask your bridal boutique what they charge for the modifications you are considering.

**Tips To Save Money:**  Consider hiring an independent tailor. Their fees are usually lower than bridal boutiques.

**Price Range:** $50 - $150


## HEADPIECE & VEIL

The headpiece is the part of the bride's outfit to which the veil is attached.

**Options for Headpieces:**  Banana Clip, Bow, Garden Hat, Headband, Juliet Cap, Mantilla, Pillbox, Pouf, Snood, Tiara.

**Options for Veils:**  Ballet, Bird Cage, Blusher, Cathedral Length, Chapel Length, Fingertip, Flyaway.

**Things To Consider:**  The headpiece should complement but not overshadow your gown.  In addition to the headpiece, you might want a veil.  Veils come in different styles and lengths.  Select a length which complements the length of your train.  Consider the total look you're trying to achieve with your gown, headpiece, veil, and hairstyle.

**Tips To Save Money:**  Some boutiques offer a free headpiece or veil with the purchase of a gown.  Make sure you ask for this before purchasing your gown.

**Price Range:** $60 - $250

## GLOVES

Gloves add a nice touch with either short-sleeved, three-quarter length, or sleeveless gowns.

**Options:** Gloves come in various styles and lengths. Depending on the length of your sleeves, select gloves that reach above your elbow, just below your elbow, halfway between your wrist and elbow, or only to your wrist. Fingerless mitts are another option that you may want to consider.

**Things To Consider:** You may want to consider fingerless mitts which allow the groom to place the wedding ring on your ring finger without having to remove your glove. You should not wear gloves if your gown has long sleeves, or if you're planning a small, at-home wedding.

**Price Range:** $5 - $30


## JEWELRY

You will need to decide what jewelry to wear on your wedding day: earrings, necklace, bracelet and/or rings.

**Options:** Select pieces of jewelry that can be classified as "something old, something new, something borrowed, or something blue" (see page 161)

**Things To Consider:** Brides look best with just a few pieces of jewelry -- perhaps a string of pearls and earrings. You certainly don't want to draw attention away from your lovely gown.

**Price Range:** $60 - $1,000

## STOCKINGS

Stockings should be selected with care, especially if the groom will be removing a garter from your leg at the reception.

**Things To Consider:**  Consider having your maid of honor carry an extra pair, just in case you get a run.

**Price Range:**  $5 - $15

## GARTER

It is customary for the bride to wear a garter just above or below the knee on her wedding day.  After the bouquet tossing ceremony, the groom takes the garter off the bride's leg.  All the single men gather on the dance floor.  The groom then tosses the garter to them over his back.  According to age-old tradition, whoever catches the garter is the next to be married!

**Things To Consider:**  You will need to choose the proper music for this event.  A popular and fun song to play during the garter removal ceremony is *The Stripper,* by David Rose.

**Price Range:**  $5 - $15

## SHOES

**Things To Consider:**  Make sure you select comfortable shoes that complement your gown;  and don't forget to break them in well before your wedding day.  Tight shoes can make you miserable and ruin your wedding day!

**Price Range:**  $25 -$100

## HAIRDRESSER

Many brides prefer to have their hair professionally arranged with their headpiece the day of the wedding rather than trying to do it themselves.

**Things To Consider:**   If you decide to use a professional hairdresser the day of your wedding, be sure to have him/her experiment with your hair and headpiece before your wedding day so that there are no surprises.  On your wedding day, you can either go to the salon or have the stylist meet you at your home or dressing site.  Consider having him/her arrange your mother's and your bridesmaids' hair for a consistent look.

**Tips To Save Money:**  Try to negotiate having your hair arranged free of charge or at a discount in exchange for bringing your mother, your fiancé's mother and your wedding party to the salon.

**Price Range:**  $20 - $75 per person

## MAKEUP ARTIST

Many brides prefer to have their makeup professionally applied on their wedding day rather than trying to do it themselves.

**Things To Consider:**   It's smart to go for a trial run before the day of the wedding so that there are no surprises.  You can either go to the salon or have the makeup artist meet you at your home or dressing site.  Consider having him/her apply makeup for your mother, your fiancé's mother and your bridesmaids for a consistent look.  In selecting a makeup artist, make sure s/he has been trained in makeup for photography.  It is very important to wear the proper amount of makeup for photographs.

**Tips To Save Money:**    Try to negotiate having your makeup applied free of charge or at a discount in exchange for bringing your mother, your fiancé's mother and your wedding party to the salon.

**Price Range:**  $15 - $75 per person

## MANICURE / PEDICURE

As a final touch, it's nice to have a professional manicure and/or pedicure the day of your wedding.

**Things To Consider:**    Don't forget to bring the appropriate color nail polish with you for your appointment.  You can either go to the salon or have the manicurist meet you at your home or dressing site.   Consider having him/her give your mother, your fiancé's mother and your bridesmaids a manicure in the same color for a consistent look.

**Tips To Save Money:**    Try to negotiate getting a manicure or pedicure free of charge or at a discount in exchange for bringing your mother, your fiancé's mother and your wedding party to the salon.

**Price Range:**  $10 - $30 per person

## GROOM'S FORMAL WEAR

The groom should select his formal wear based on the formality of the wedding.  For a semi-formal or formal wedding, the groom will need a tuxedo.  A tuxedo is the formal jacket worn by men on special or formal occasions.  Popular colors are black, white, and gray.

**Options:**  Use the following guidelines to select customary attire for the groom:

**Informal wedding:**   Business suit
White dress shirt and tie

**Semi-formal daytime:**   Formal suit
White dress shirt
Cummerbund or vest
Four-in-hand or bow tie

**Semi-formal evening:**   Formal suit or dinner jacket
Matching trousers
White shirt
Cummerbund or vest
Black bow tie
Cufflinks and studs

**Formal daytime:**   Cutaway or stroller jacket
Waistcoat
Striped trousers
White wing-collared shirt
Striped tie
Studs and cufflinks

**Formal evening:**   Black dinner jacket
Matching trousers
Waistcoat
White tuxedo shirt
Bow tie
Cummerbund or vest
Cufflinks

**Very formal daytime:**   Cutaway coat
Wing-collared shirt

Ascot
Striped trousers
Cufflinks
Gloves

**Very formal evening:**    Black tailcoat
Matching striped trousers
Bow tie
White wing-collared shirt
Waistcoat
Patent leather shoes
Studs and cufflinks
Gloves

**Things To Consider:**  In selecting your formal wear, keep in mind the formality of your wedding, the time of day,  and the bride's gown.   Consider darker colors for a fall or winter wedding and lighter colors for a spring or summer wedding.   When selecting a place to rent your tuxedo,  check the reputation of the shop.  Make sure they have a wide variety of makes and styles to choose from.

Reserve tuxedos for yourself and your ushers several weeks before the wedding to insure a wide selection and to allow enough time for alterations.   Plan to pick up the tuxedos a few days before the wedding to allow time for last minute alterations in case they don't fit properly.  Out-of-town men in your wedding party can be sized at any tuxedo shop.  They can send their measurements to you or directly to the shop where you are going to rent your tuxedos.

Ask about the store's return policy and be sure you delegate to the appropriate person (usually your best man) the responsibility of returning all tuxedos within the time allotted.  Ushers customarily pay for their own tuxedos.

**Tips To Save Money:**　Try to negotiate getting your tuxedo for free or at a discount in exchange for having your father, your fiancé's father and ushers rent their tuxedos at that shop.

**Price Range:**　$60 - $120

# PHOTOGRAPHY

## BRIDE & GROOM'S ALBUM

The bride and groom's photo album is the best way to preserve your special day. Chances are you and your fiancé will look at the photos many times during your lifetime. Therefore, hiring a good photographer is one of the most important tasks in planning your wedding.

**Options:** There are a large variety of wedding albums. They vary in size, color, material, construction and price. Find one that you like and will feel proud of showing to your friends and family. Some of the most popular manufacturers of wedding albums are Art Leather, Leather Craftsman and Renaissance.

Make sure you review the differences between these albums before selecting one. You will also need to select the finish process of your photos. Ask your photographer to show you samples of various finishes. Some of the most popular finishes are glossy, lustre, semi-matte, pebble finish, spray texture and oil.

**Things To Consider:** Make sure you hire a photographer who specializes in weddings. Your photographer should be experienced in wedding procedures and familiar with your ceremony and reception sites. This will allow him/her to anticipate your next move and be in the proper place at the right time to capture all the special moments. Personal rapport is extremely important. The photographer may be an expert, but if you don't feel comfortable or at ease with him or her, your photography will reflect this. Comfort and compatibility with your photographer can make or break your wedding day and your photographs!

Look at his/her work. See if the photographer captured the excitement and emotion of the bridal couple. Also, remember that the wedding album should unfold like a story book -- the story of your wedding. Be sure to discuss with your photographer the photos you want so that there is no misunderstanding. A good wedding photographer should have a list of suggested poses to choose from. Some of the more popular poses are:

**A)** **Pre-Ceremony Photos:**

Wedding rings with the invitation.
Bride getting dressed for the ceremony.
Bride looking at her bridal bouquet.
Maid of honor putting garter on bride's leg.
Groom and best man before ceremony.
Bride with her parents.
Bride with her entire family and/or any combination thereof.
Bride with her bridesmaids.
Bride with the flower girl and/or ring bearer.
Groom with his parents.
Groom with his entire family and/or any combination thereof.
Groom with his ushers.
Groom with the bride's father.
Bride and her father, before walking down the aisle.

**B)** **Ceremony Photos:**

Bride and groom saying their vows.
Bride and groom exchanging rings.
Groom kissing the bride at the altar.

Newlyweds with both of their families.
Newlyweds with the entire wedding party.
Bride and groom signing the marriage certificate.
Musicians.
Receiving Line.

## C)    Reception Photos:

Grand entrance of newlyweds and their wedding party into
  the reception site.
Cake table.
Toasts.
First dance.
Cake-cutting ceremony.
Bouquet-tossing ceremony.
Garter-tossing ceremony.
Newlyweds leaving the reception for their honeymoon.
Candid shots of your guests.

Look at albums ready to be delivered, or proofs of weddings
recently photographed. Look at the photographer's preferred style.
Some photographers are known for formal poses, while others
specialize in more candid, creative shots. Some can do both.

When asked to provide references, many photographers will give
you the names of people they know are happy with their work.
Some may even give you names from weddings they performed
several years ago. This may not indicate the photographer's current
ability or reputation. So when asking for references, be sure to ask
for recent weddings the photographer has performed. This will
give you a good idea of his/her current work. Be sure to ask if the
photographer was prompt, cordial, properly dressed and whether
s/he performed his/her duties as expected.

When comparing prices, consider the number, size and finish of the photographs and the type of album the photographer will use. Ask how many proofs you will get to choose your photos from. The more proofs, the better the selection you will have. Some photographers do not work with proofs. Rather, they simply supply you with a finished album after the wedding. Doing this may reduce the cost of your album but will also reduce your selection of photographs.

**Questions To Ask:** Make sure you ask all the following questions to ensure a smart hiring decision:

- How many years of experience do you have as a professional wedding photographer?
- What percentage of your total photography business is dedicated to weddings?
- Approximately how many weddings have you photographed?
- Are you the person who will photograph my wedding?
- Will you bring an assistant with you to my wedding?
- How do you typically dress for weddings?
- Do you have a professional studio?
- What type of equipment do you use?
- Do you bring backup equipment with you to weddings?
- Do you visit the ceremony and reception sites prior to the wedding?
- Do you have liability insurance?
- Are you skilled in diffused lighting & soft focus?
- Can you take studio portraits?
- Can you retouch negatives?
- Can negatives be purchased? If so, what is the cost?
- What is the cost of the package I am interested in?
- What does the desired package include?
- What is your payment policy?
- What is your cancellation policy?

- Do you offer a money-back guarantee?
- Do you use proofs?
- How many proofs will I get?
- When will I get my proofs?
- When will I get my album?
- What is the cost of an engagement portrait?
- What is the cost of a parent album?
- What is the cost of a 5" x 7" reprint?
- What is the cost of an 8" x 10" reprint?
- What is the cost of an 11" x 14" reprint?
- What is the cost per additional hour of shooting at the wedding?

**Beware:** Make sure the photographer you interview is the one who will photograph your wedding. There are many companies with more than one photographer. Often these companies use the work of the best photographer to sell their packages and then send a less experienced photographer to the wedding. Don't get caught in this trap! Be sure you meet with the photographer who will shoot your wedding. This way you can get an idea of his/her style and personality.

Also, some churches do not allow photographs to be shot during the ceremony. Make sure your photographer understands the rules and regulations of your church before planning the ceremony shots.

**Tips To Save Money:**    Consider hiring a professional photographer for the formal shots of your ceremony only. You can then place disposable cameras on each table at the reception and let your guests take candid shots. This can save you a considerable amount of money in photography.

You can also lower the price of your album by paying for the photographs and then putting them into the album yourself. This is a very time-consuming task, so your photographer may reduce the price of his/her package if you opt to do this. To really economize, select a photographer who charges a flat fee to shoot the wedding and will allow you to purchase the film.

Compare at least 3 photographers for quality, value and price. Photographers who shoot weddings "on the side" are usually less expensive than professional wedding photographers.

Select a few 8" x 10"s for your album and more 4" x 5"s, and choose a moderately priced album. Ask for specials and package deals.

**Price Range:**   $400 - $3000

## PARENTS' ALBUM

The parents' album is a smaller version of the bride and groom's album. It usually contains about twenty 5" x 7" photographs. Photos should be carefully selected for each individual family. If given as a gift, the album can be personalized with the bride and groom's names and date of the wedding on the front cover.

**Tips To Save Money:** Try to negotiate at least one free parents' album with the purchase of the bride and groom's album.

**Price Range:** $60 - $300

## EXTRA PRINTS

Extra prints are photographs ordered in addition to the main album or parents' album. These are usually purchased as gifts for the bridal party, close friends and family members.

**Things To Consider:**  It is important to discuss the cost of extra prints since prices vary considerably.  Some photographers offer the main album at great bargains to get the job, but then charge a fortune on extra prints.  Think how many extra prints you would like to order and figure this into your budget before selecting your photographer.

**Tips To Save Money:**  Ask your photographer to sell you the negatives.  It's always less expensive to have the negatives developed into prints yourself than to order them from a professional photographer.

If you can wait, consider not ordering any reprints during the first few years after the wedding.  A few years later, contact the photographer and ask if s/he will sell you the negatives.  Most photographers will be glad to sell them at a bargain price.  You can then make as many prints as you wish for a fraction of the cost.

**Price Range:**  (5" x 7") = $3 - $15;   (8" x 10") = $10 - $25;   (11" x 14") = $25 - $75

## PROOFS / PREVIEWS

Proofs/previews are the preliminary prints from which the bride and groom select photographs for their album and for their parents' albums.  They are normally 5" x 5" in size.

**Things To Consider:**  When selecting a package, ask how many proofs the photographer will take.  The more proofs, the wider the selection you will have to choose from.  For a wide selection, the photographer must take at least 2 to 3 times the number of prints that will go into your album.

Ask the photographer how soon after the wedding you will get your proofs. Request this in writing. The proofs should be ready by the time you get back from your honeymoon. Also request to see your proofs before you make the final payment.

**Tips To Save Money:** Ask your photographer to use your proofs as part of your album package to save developing costs.

**Price Range:** $100 - $600

## NEGATIVES

Negatives come in different sizes depending on the type of film and equipment used. The most popular camera for weddings is the medium format camera. When a medium format camera is used, the size of the negatives is 2 1/4" x 2 1/4." When a 35 mm camera is used, the negatives are only 1" x 1 1/2." The larger the negative, the higher the quality of the photograph, especially when enlarged. Don't let a photographer convince you that there is no difference in quality between a 35 mm camera and a medium format camera.

**Things To Consider:** Most photographers will not sell you the negatives since they hope to make a profit on selling extra prints after the wedding. Ask the photographers you interview how long they keep the negatives. A professional photographer should keep the negatives at least five years. Make sure you get this in writing.

**Tips To Save Money:** Purchasing the negatives will save you a lot of money when duplicating prints for family and friends. But don't spend money on purchasing negatives unless you are planning to make a lot of reprints. If you can wait, consider not buying the negatives right away. Contact the photographer a few years later and ask if s/he will sell you the negatives.  Most photographers will be glad to sell them at a bargain price.

**Price Range:**  $100 - $800

## ENGAGEMENT PHOTOGRAPH

The engagement photograph is sent to your local newspapers, along with information announcing your engagement to the public. This announcement is usually made by the bride's parents or her immediate family.

**Things To Consider:**    The photograph (usually in black and white) was traditionally of the bride alone, but today is usually of the engaged couple.

**Tips To Save Money:**  Look at engagement photographs in your local newspaper.   Then have a friend or family member take a photograph of you and your fiancé in a pose similar to the ones you have seen.

**Price Range:**  $35 - $75

## FORMAL BRIDAL PORTRAIT

If you intend to announce your marriage in the newspaper the day after your wedding, you will need to have a formal bridal portrait taken several weeks before the wedding.  This is a photograph of the bride taken before the wedding in the photographer's studio. This photograph, along with an announcement, must be sent to your local newspapers as soon as possible.

**Things To Consider:**  Some fine bridal salons provide an attractive background where the bride may arrange to have her formal bridal photograph taken after the final fitting of her gown.  This will save you the hassle of bringing your gown and headpiece to the photographer's studio and dressing up once again.

**Tips To Save Money:**    If you don't mind announcing your marriage several weeks after the wedding, consider having your formal portrait taken the day of your wedding.  This will save you the studio costs, the hassle of getting dressed for the photo, and the photograph will be more natural since the bridal bouquet will be the one you actually carried down the aisle.  Also, brides are always most beautiful on their wedding day!

**Price Range:**  $50 - $150

# VIDEOGRAPHY

## MAIN VIDEO

Next to your photo album, videography is the best way to preserve your wedding memories. Unlike photographs, videography captures the mood of the wedding day in motion and sound. You have the option of selecting one, two, or three cameras. The more cameras used, the more action captured and the more expensive. An experienced videographer, however, can do a good job with just one camera.

**Options:** There are various types of video cameras available. Commercial cameras are the best. These are used for television and special events. The next best cameras are Super VHS followed by Super 8 mm. Compare videographer's equipment when comparing their packages and prices. And don't forget to ask if your videographer has a wireless microphone. It will come in handy during the ceremony when you want to capture all the words at a distance without the need for a long cable.

**Things To Consider:** Look at previous weddings the videographer has videotaped. Notice the color and brightness of the screen, as well as the quality of the sound. This will indicate the quality of his/her equipment. Notice the picture -- is it smooth or jerky? This will indicate the videographer's level of skill. Notice any special effects such as titles, dissolve, and multiple screens.

Make sure you hire someone who specializes in weddings. Just like your photographer, your videographer should be experienced in wedding procedures and, ideally, should be familiar with the layout of your ceremony and reception sites. This will allow him/her to anticipate your next move and be in the proper place at the right time to capture all the special moments.

Remember to ask your videographer to interview your wedding party, close friends and family members, asking them to make a wish or toast to both of you as a married couple, or to tell any "wild" stories they may want to share for the record. This personalizes your video and is a wonderful memento. Consider both personality and professionalism when hiring your videographer.

Find out what is included in each package you are considering: hours of coverage, titling, in-camera editing or post-editing. If you will be getting married in a church, find out the church's policies regarding videography. Some churches do not allow a videographer to be close to the ceremony.

To preserve your wedding video for years to come, store it in a cool, dark place away from dust and dirt.

**Questions To Ask:** Make sure you ask all the following questions to ensure a smart hiring decision:

* How many years of experience do you have as a professional wedding videographer?
* Approximately how many weddings have you taped?
* Are you the person who will videotape my wedding?
* Will you bring an assistant with you to my wedding?
* How do you dress for weddings?
* Do you have professional editing equipment?
* What type of equipment do you use?

- Do you have a wireless microphone?
- Can you videotape in low light?
- What format do you use (VHS, Super VHS, 8mm)?
- Do you bring backup equipment with you?
- Do you visit the ceremony and reception sites before the wedding?
- Do you edit the tape after the event?
- Who keeps the raw footage?
- When will I receive the final product?
- Can you make a photo montage?  If so, at what price?
- What is the cost of the package I am interested in?
- What does the desired package include?
- What is your payment policy?
- What is your cancellation policy?
- Do you offer a money-back guarantee?

**Beware:**  As in photography, there are many companies with more than one videographer.  These companies often use the work of the best videographer to sell their packages and then send a less experienced videographer to the wedding.  Again, don't get caught in this trap!  Be sure to interview the videographer who will shoot your wedding so you can get a good idea of his/her style and personality.  Ask to see his/her own work.

**Tips To Save Money:**  Compare videographers' quality, value and price.  There is a wide range, and the most expensive is not necessarily the best.  One camera is the most cost effective and may be all you need.  Consider hiring a company that offers both videography and photography.  You may save overall.

Ask a family member or close friend to videotape your wedding.  However, realize that without professional equipment and expertise the final product may not be quite the same.

**Price Range:**  $350 - $2,000

## TITLES

Titles and subtitles can be edited into your video before or after the filming. Titles are important since twenty years from now you might not remember the exact time of your wedding or the names of your wedding party members. Some videographers charge more for titling. Make sure you discuss this with your videographer and get in writing exactly what titles will be included.

**Options:** Titles may include the date, time and location of the wedding, the bride and groom's names, and names of special family members and/or the wedding party. Titles may also include special thanks to those who helped with the wedding. You can send these people a copy of your video after the wedding. This is a very appropriate and inexpensive gift!

**Tips To Save Money:** Consider borrowing a camera with a character generator from a friend and doing the titling yourself.

**Price Range:** $40 - $75

## EXTRA HOURS

Find out how much your videographer would charge to stay longer than contracted for in your original package. If this is not disclosed, a videographer can charge a fortune if asked to stay longer. Don't forget to get this in writing.

**Tips To Save Money:** Avoid paying extra hours beyond what's included in your selected package. You can do this by calculating the number of hours you think you'll need and negotiating that into your package price. Consider taping the ceremony only. ·Eliminate the extras such as titles and photo montage. You can do this yourself.

**Price Range:**  $35 - $60/hour

## PHOTO MONTAGE

A photo montage is a series of photographs set to music on video. The number of photographs depends on the length of the song and the amount of time allotted for each photograph. A typical song usually allows for approximately 40 to 50 photographs. Photo montages are a great way to reproduce your photographs. Copies of this video can be made for considerably less than the cost of reproducing photographs.

**Options:**  Photo montages can be made of you and your fiancé growing up, the rehearsal, the wedding day, the honeymoon, or any combination thereof.

**Things To Consider:**  Send copies of your photo montage video to close friends and family members as mementos of your wedding.

**Tips To Save Money:**  Consider making a photo montage yourself. This is very easily done with any video camera, a tripod, and a good stereo. The secret is in holding the camera very still and having the proper lighting while videotaping the photographs.

**Price Range:**  $50 - $100

## EXTRA COPIES

A professional videographer will be able to reproduce your video much easier and better than you can, provided s/he has professional equipment. Be sure to ask your videographer how much s/he charges for extra copies of the wedding videotape. You'll certainly want to give your parents a copy!

**Tips To Save Money:**　Borrow a VCR from a friend and make copies yourself.

**Price Range:**　$5 - $35

# STATIONERY

## INVITATIONS

Begin creating your guest list as soon as possible. Ask your parents and the groom's parents for a list of the people they would like to invite. You and your fiancé should make your own list. Make certain that all names are spelled correctly and that all addresses are current. Determine if you wish to include children; if so, add their names to your list. All children over the age of 16 should receive their own invitation.

Order your invitations at least 4 months before the wedding. Allow an additional month for engraved invitations. Invitations are traditionally issued by the bride's parents; but if the groom's parents are assuming some of the wedding costs, the invitations should be in their names also. Mail all invitations at the same time, 6 - 8 weeks before the wedding.

**Options:** There are three types of invitations: traditional/formal, contemporary, and informal. The traditional/formal wedding invitation is white, soft cream, or ivory with raised black lettering. The printing is done on the top page of a double sheet of thick quality paper; the inside is left blank. The contemporary invitation is typically an individualized presentation that makes a statement about the bride and groom. Informal invitations are often printed on the front of a single, heavyweight card and may be handwritten or preprinted.

There are three types of printing: engraved, thermography, and offset printing. Engraving is the most expensive, traditional and formal type of printing. It also takes the longest to complete. In engraved printing, stationery is pressed onto a copper plate, which makes the letters rise slightly from the page. Thermography is a process that fuses powder and ink to create a raised letter. This takes less time than engraving and is less expensive because copper plates do not have to be engraved. Offset printing, the least expensive, is the quickest to produce and offers a variety of styles and colors. It is also the least formal.

**Things To Consider:** If all your guests are to be invited to both the ceremony and the reception, a combined invitation may be sent without separate enclosure cards. Order one invitation for each married or cohabiting couple that you plan to invite. The officiant and his/her spouse as well as your attendants should receive an invitation.

Order approximately 20% more stationery than your actual head count. Allow a minimum of two weeks to address and mail the invitations, longer if using a calligrapher or if your guest list is very large. You may also want to consider ordering invitations to the rehearsal dinner, as these should be in the same style as the wedding invitation.

## SAMPLES OF TRADITIONAL/FORMAL INVITATIONS

**1)     When the bride's parents sponsor the wedding:**

Mr. and Mrs. Alexander Waterman Smith
request the honor of your presence
at the marriage of their daughter

Carol Ann
to
Mr. William James Clark
on Saturday, the twenty-seventh of May
two thousand
at three o'clock in the afternoon
Saint James by-the-Sea
La Jolla, California


2)      **When the groom's parents sponsor the wedding:**

Mr. and Mrs. Michael Burdell Clark
request the honor of your presence
at the marriage of
Miss Carol Ann Smith
to their son
Mr. William James Clark


3)      **When both the bride and groom's parents**
        **sponsor  the wedding:**

Mr. and Mrs. Alexander Waterman Smith
and
Mr. and Mrs. Michael Burdell Clark
request the honor of your presence
at the marriage of their children
Miss Carol Ann Smith
to
Mr. William James Clark

OR

Mr. and Mrs. Alexander Waterman Smith
request the honor of your presence
at the marriage of their daughter
Carol Ann Smith
to
William James Clark
son of Mr. and Mrs. Michael Burdell Clark

**4)   When the bride and groom sponsor their own wedding:**

The honor of your presence is requested
at the marriage of
Miss Carol Ann Smith
and
Mr. William James Clark

OR

Miss Carol Ann Smith
and
Mr. William James Clark
request the honor of your presence
at their marriage

**5)   With divorced or deceased parents:**

When the bride's mother is sponsoring the wedding and is not remarried:

Mrs. Julie Hurden Smith
requests the honor of your presence

at the marriage of her daughter
Carol Ann

When the bride's mother is sponsoring and has remarried:

Mrs. Julie Hurden Booker
requests the honor of your presence
at the marriage of her daughter
Carol Ann Smith

OR

Mr. and Mrs. John Thomas Booker
request the honor of your presence
at the marriage of Mrs. Booker's daughter
Carol Ann Smith

When the bride's father is sponsoring the wedding and has not remarried:

Mr. Alexander Waterman Smith
requests the honor of your presence
at the marriage of his daughter
Carol Ann

When the bride's father is sponsoring and has remarried:

Mr. and Mrs. Alexander Waterman Smith
request the honor of your presence
at the marriage of Mr. Smith's daughter
Carol Ann

### 6)   Deceased parents:

Both parents are deceased and a close friend or relative sponsors
the wedding:

> Mr. and Mrs. Brandt Elliott Lawson
> request the honor of your presence
> at the marriage of their granddaughter
> Carol Ann Smith

### 7)   In military ceremonies, the rank determines the placement of names:

Any title lower than sergeant should be omitted.  Only the branch of
service should be included under that person's name:

> Mr. and Mrs. Alexander Waterman Smith
> request the honor of your presence
> at the marriage of their daughter
> Carol Ann
> United States Army
> to
> William James Clark

Junior officers' titles are placed below their names and are followed
by their branch of service:

> Mr. and Mrs. Alexander Waterman Smith
> request the honor of your presence
> at the marriage of their daughter
> Carol Ann
> to

William James Clark
First Lieutenant, United States Army


If the rank is higher than lieutenant, titles are placed before names, and the branch of service is placed on the following line:


Mr. and Mrs. Alexander Waterman Smith
request the honor of your presence
at the marriage of their daughter
Carol Ann
to
Captain William James Clark
United States Navy


## SAMPLE OF A LESS FORMAL, MORE CONTEMPORARY INVITATION

Mr. and Mrs. Alexander Waterman Smith
would like you to
join with their daughter
Carol Ann
and
William James Clark
in the celebration of their marriage


**Tips To Save Money:** Thermography looks like engraving and is one-third the cost. Choose paper stock that is reasonable and yet achieves your overall look. Select invitations that can be mailed with a single stamp. Order at least 25 extra invitations, just in case you add people to your list or mess some up. To reorder this small number of invitations later would cost nearly three times the amount you'll spend up front.

**Price Range:** $0.75 - $5 per invitation

## RESPONSE CARDS

Response cards are enclosed with the invitation to determine the number of people who will be attending your wedding. They are the smallest card size accepted by the postal service and should be printed in the same style as the invitation. An invitation to only the wedding ceremony does not usually include a request for a reply. However, response cards should be used when it is necessary to have an exact head count for special seating arrangements. Response cards are widely accepted today. If included, these cards should be easy for your guests to understand and use. Include a self-addressed and stamped return envelope to make it easy for your guests to return the response cards.

**Things To Consider:** You should not include a line that reads "number of persons" on your response cards because only those whose names appear on the inner and outer envelopes are invited. Each couple, each single person, and all children over the age of 16 should receive their own invitation. Indicate on the inner envelope if they may bring an escort or guest. The omitting of children's names from the inner envelope infers that the children are not invited.

Samples of wording for response cards:

M_____

(The M may be eliminated from the line, especially if many Drs. are invited)

____ accepts

____ regrets

Saturday the fifth of July

Oceanside Country Club

OR

The favor of your reply is requested
by the twenty-second of May
M_____
will _____ attend

**Price Range:**   $.40 - $.80 each

## RECEPTION CARDS

If the guest list for the ceremony is larger than that for the
reception, a separate card with the date, time and location for the
reception should be enclosed with the ceremony invitation for those
guests also invited to the reception.   Reception cards should be
placed in front of the invitation, facing the back flap and the person
inserting them.   They should be printed on the same quality paper
and in the same style as the invitation itself.

Sample of a formally-worded reception card:

Mr. and Mrs. Alexander Waterman Smith
request the pleasure of your company
Saturday, the third of July
at three o'clock
Oceanside Country Club
2020 Waterview Lane
Oceanside, California

Sample of a less formal reception card:

Reception immediately following the ceremony
Oceanside Country Club
2020 Waterview Lane
Oceanside, California

**Things To Consider:**  You may also include a reception card in all your invitations if the reception is to be held at a different site than the ceremony.

**Tips To Save Money:**  If all people invited to the ceremony are also invited to the reception, include the reception information on the invitation and eliminate the reception card.  This will save printing and postage costs.

**Price Range:**  $.35 - $.60 each

## CEREMONY CARDS

If the guest list for the reception is larger than the guest list for the ceremony, a special insertion card with the date, time and location for the ceremony should be enclosed with the reception invitation for those guests also invited to the ceremony.

Ceremony cards should be placed in front of the invitation, facing the back flap and the person inserting them.  They should be printed on the same quality paper and in the same style as the invitation itself.

**Price Range:**    $.35 - $.60 each

## PEW CARDS

Pew cards may be used to let special guests and family members know they are to be seated in the reserved section on either the bride's side or the groom's side.  These are most typically seen in large, formal ceremonies.  Guests should take this card to the ceremony and show it to the ushers, who should then escort them to their seats.

**Options:**  Pew cards may indicate a specific pew number if specific seats are assigned, or may read "Within the Ribbon" if a certain number of pews are reserved but no specific seat is assigned.

**Things To Consider:**  Pew cards may be inserted along with the invitation, or may be sent separately after the RSVPs have been returned.  It is often easier to send them after you have received all RSVPs so you know how many reserved pews will be needed.

**Tips To Save Money:**  Include the pew card with the invitation and just say "Within the Ribbon."  After you have received all your RSVPs, you will know how many pews will need to be reserved for these special guests.  This will save you the cost of mailing the pew cards separately.

**Price Range:**  $.20 - $.60 each

## SEATING / PLACE CARDS

Seating/place cards are used to let guests know where they should be seated at the reception and are a good way of putting people together so they feel most comfortable.  Place cards should be laid out alphabetically on a table at the entrance to the reception.  Each card should correspond to a table -- either by number, color, or other identifying factor.  Each table should be marked accordingly.

**Options:**   Select a traditional or contemporary design for your place cards, depending on the style of your wedding.
Regardless of the design, place cards must contain the same information:  the bride and groom's names on the first line; the date on the second line; the third line is left blank for you to write in the guest's name; and the fourth line is for the table number, color, or other identifying factor.

**Price Range:**  $.20 - $.60 each

## RAIN CARDS

These cards are enclosed when guests are invited to an outdoor ceremony and/or reception, informing them of an alternate location in case of bad weather.  As with other enclosures, rain cards should be placed in front of the invitation, facing the back flap and the person inserting them.  They should be printed on the same quality paper and in the same style as the invitation itself.

**Price Range:**  $.20 - $.30 each

## MAPS

Maps to the ceremony and/or reception are becoming frequent inserts in wedding invitations.  They need to be drawn and printed in the same style as the invitation and are usually on a small, heavier card.  If they are not printed in the same style or on the same type of paper as the invitation, they should be mailed separately.

**Options:** Maps should include both written and visual instructions, keeping in mind the fact that guests may be coming from different locations.

**Things To Consider:**    Order extra maps to hand out at the ceremony if the reception is at a different location.

**Tips To Save Money:** If you are comfortable with computers, you can purchase software that allows you to draw your own maps. Print a map to both the ceremony and reception on the same sheet of paper, perhaps one on each side.  This will save you the cost of mailing two maps.  Or have your ushers hand out maps to the reception after the ceremony.

**Price Range:** $.50 - $.75 each

## CEREMONY PROGRAMS

Ceremony programs are printed documents showing the sequence of events during the ceremony.  These programs add a personal touch to your wedding and are a convenient way of letting guests know who your attendants, officiant, and ceremony musicians are. For example:

The Marriage of
Carol Ann Smith and William James Clark
the fourth of March, 2000
San Diego, California

**Our Ceremony**

Prelude:
*All I Ask of You*, by Andrew Lloyd Webber

Processional:
*The Canon*, by Pachelbel

Rite of Marriage

Welcome guests

Statement of intentions

Marriage vows

Exchange of rings

Blessing of bride and groom

Pronouncement of marriage

Presentation of the bride and groom

Recessional:
*Trumpet Voluntary*, by Jeromiah Clarke

**Our Wedding Party**

Maid of Honor:
Susan Smith, Sister of Bride

Best Man:
Brandt Clark, Brother of Groom

Bridesmaids:
Janet Anderson, Friend of Bride
Lisa Bennett, Friend of Bride

Ushers:
Mark Gleason, Friend of Groom
Tommy Olson, Friend of Groom

Officiant:
Father Henry Thomas

**Our Reception**

Please join us after the ceremony
in the celebration of our marriage at:
La Valencia Hotel
1132 Prospect Street
La Jolla, CA

**Options:**  Ceremony programs can be handed out to guests by the ushers, or they can be placed at the back of the church for guests to take as they enter.

**Price Range:**  $.75 - $1.75 each

## ANNOUNCEMENTS

Announcements are not obligatory but do serve a useful purpose. They may be sent to those friends who are not invited to the wedding because the number of guests must be limited, or because they live too far away. They may also be sent to acquaintances who, while not particularly close to the family, might still wish to know of the marriage.

Announcements are also appropriate for friends and acquaintances who are not expected to attend and for whom you do not want to give an obligation of sending a gift. They should include the day, month, year, city, and state where the ceremony took place.

**Things To Consider:** Announcements should never be sent to anyone who has received an invitation to the ceremony or the reception. They are printed on the same paper and in the same style as the invitations. They should be addressed before the wedding and mailed the day of or the day after the ceremony.

**Price Range:** $.50 - $1

## THANK-YOU NOTES

Regardless of whether the bride has thanked the donor in person or not, she must write a thank-you note for every gift received.

**Things To Consider:** Order thank-you notes along with your other stationery at least four months before your wedding. You should order some with your maiden initials for thank-you notes sent before the ceremony, and the rest with your married initials for notes sent after the wedding and for future use. Send thank-you notes within two weeks of receiving a gift that arrives before the wedding, and within two months after the honeymoon for gifts received on or after your wedding day. Be sure to mention the gift you received in the body of the note and let the person know how much you like it and what you and your spouse plan to do with it.

**Price Range:** $.30 - $.50

## STAMPS

Don't forget to budget stamps for response cards as well as for invitations!

**Things To Consider:**  Don't order your stamps until you have had the post office weigh your completed invitation. It may exceed the size and weight for one stamp. Order commemorative stamps that fit the occasion.

**Price Range:**  $.33 - $1

# CALLIGRAPHY

Calligraphy is a form of elegant handwriting often used to address invitations for formal occasions. Traditional wedding invitations should be addressed by hand in black or blue fountain pen.

**Options:**  You may address the invitations yourself, hire a professional calligrapher, or have your invitations addressed using calligraphy by computer. Make sure you use the same method or person to address both the inner and outer envelopes.

**Tips To Save Money:**  You may want to consider taking a short course to learn the art of calligraphy so that you can address your own invitations. If you have a computer with a laser printer, you can also address the invitations yourself using calligraphy fonts. There are many beautiful styles to choose from.

**Price Range:**  $.30 - $3 each

# NAPKINS AND MATCHBOOKS

Napkins and matchbooks may also be ordered from your stationer. These are placed around the reception room as decorative items and mementos of the event.

**Things To Consider:**  Napkins and matchbooks can be printed in your wedding colors or white with gold or silver lettering.  Include both of your names and the wedding date.  You may consider including a phrase or thought, or a small graphic design above your names.

**Price Range:**   $.5 - $1.50 each

#  ADDRESSING ENVELOPES

Use the following guidelines for addressing invitations:

## Husband and Wife  (with same surname)

**Inner Envelope**
Mr. and Mrs. Smith

**Outer Envelope**
Mr. and Mrs. Thomas Smith
(use middle name, if known)

## Husband and Wife  (with different surnames)

**Inner Envelope**
Ms. Banks and Mr. Smith
(wife first)

**Outer Envelope**
Ms. Angela Banks
Mr. Thomas Smith
(wife's name above husband's)

## Husband and Wife  (wife has professional title)

**Inner Envelope**
Dr. Smith and Mr. Smith

**Outer Envelope**
Dr. Anita Smith
Mr. Thomas Smith
(wife's name & title above husband's)

## Husband and Wife With Children under 16

**Inner Envelope**
Mr. and Mrs. Smith
John, Mary, and Glen
(in order of age)

**Outer Envelope**
Mr. and Mrs. Thomas Smith

## Single Woman  (regardless of age)

**Inner Envelope**
Miss/Ms. Smith

**Outer Envelope**
Miss/Ms. Beverly Smith

## Single Woman and Guest

**Inner Envelope**
Miss/Ms. Smith
Mr. Jones (or "and Guest")

**Outer Envelope**
Miss/Ms. Beverly Smith

Single Man

**Inner Envelope**
Mr. Jones
(Master for a young boy)

**Outer Envelope**
Mr. William Jones

Single Man and Guest

**Inner Envelope**
Mr. Jones
Miss/Ms. Smith (or "and Guest")

**Outer Envelope**
Mr. William Jones

Unmarried Couple Living Together

**Inner Envelope**
Mr. Knight and Ms. Orlandi
(names listed alphabetically)

**Outer Envelope**
Mr. Michael Knight
Ms. Paula Orlandi

Two Sisters (over 16)

**Inner Envelope**
The Misses Smith

**Outer Envelope**
The Misses Mary and Jane Smith
(in order of age)

Two Brothers  (over 16)

**Inner Envelope**
The Messrs. Smith

**Outer Envelope**
The Messrs. John and Glen Smith
(in order of age)

Brothers & Sisters  (over 16)

**Inner Envelope**
Mary, Jane, John & Glen
(name the girls first, in order of age)
**Outer Envelope**
The Misses Smith
The Messrs. Smith
(name the girls first)

A Brother and Sister  (over 16)

**Inner Envelope**
Jane and John
(name the girl first)

**Outer Envelope**
Miss Jane Smith and Mr. John Smith
(name the girl first)

## Widow

### Inner Envelope
Mrs. Smith

### Outer Envelope
Mrs. William Smith

## Divorcee

### Inner Envelope
Mrs. Smith

### Outer Envelope
Mrs. Jones Smith
(maiden name and former husband's surname)

# Personal Notes

_____
_____
_____
_____
_____
_____
_____
_____
_____
_____
_____
_____
_____
_____
_____
_____
_____
_____
_____
_____
_____
_____
_____
_____

# RECEPTION

## RECEPTION SITE FEE

The reception is a party where all your guests come together to celebrate your new life as a married couple. It should reflect and complement the formality of your ceremony. The selection of a reception site will depend on its availability, price, proximity to the ceremony site, and the number of people it will accommodate.

There are two basic types of reception sites. The first type charges a per person fee which includes the facility, food, tables, silverware, china, and so forth. Examples: hotels, restaurants and catered yachts. The second type charges a room rental fee and you are responsible for providing the food, beverages, linens, and possibly tables and chairs. Examples: clubs, halls, parks, museums, and private homes.

The advantage of the first type is that most everything is done for you. The disadvantage, however, is that your choices of food, china, and linen are limited. Usually you are not permitted to bring in an outside caterer and must select from a predetermined menu.

**Options:** Private homes, gardens, hotels, clubs, restaurants, halls, parks, museums, yachts, and wineries are some of the more popular choices for receptions.

**Things To Consider:** When comparing the cost of different locations, consider the rental fee, food, beverages, parking, gratuity, set-up charges and the cost of rental equipment needed such as tables, chairs, canopies, and so forth. If you are planning an outdoor reception, be sure to have a backup site in case of rain.

**Questions To Ask:** Make sure you ask all the following questions before selecting a reception site:

- What is the name & phone number of my contact person?
- What dates & times are available?
- What is the maximum number of guests for a seated reception?
- What is the maximum number of guests for a cocktail reception?
- What is the reception site fee?
- What is the price range for a seated lunch?
- What is the price range for a buffet lunch?
- What is the price range for a seated dinner?
- What is the price range for a buffet dinner?
- Can we keep the left over food?
- What is the corkage fee?
- What is the cake-cutting fee?
- What is the ratio of servers to guests?
- How much time will be allotted for my reception?
- What music restrictions are there, if any?
- What alcohol restrictions are there, if any?
- Are there any restrictions for rice or rose petal-tossing?
- What room and table decorations are available?
- Is a changing room available?
- Is there handicap accessibility?
- Is a dance floor included in the site fee?
- Are tables, chairs, and linens included in the site fee?
- Are outside caterers allowed?
- Are kitchen facilities available for outside caterers?
- Does the facility have full liability insurance?
- What "perks" or giveaways are offered?

- How many parking spaces are available for my family and wedding party?
- How many parking spaces are available for my guests?
- What is the cost for parking, if any?
- What is the cost for sleeping rooms, if available?
- What is the payment policy?
- What is the cancellation policy?
- Are credit cards accepted?

**Beware:**  Some hotels are known for double booking.  A bride may reserve the largest or most elegant room in a hotel for her reception, only to find out later that the hotel took the liberty to book a more profitable event in the room she had reserved and moved her reception over to a smaller or less elegant room.

Also be careful of hotels that book events too close together.  You don't want your guests to wait outside while your room is being set up for the reception.  And you don't want to be "forced out" before you are ready to leave because the hotel needs to arrange the room for the next reception.  Get your rental hours and the name of your room in writing.

**Tips To Save Money:**    Since the cost of the reception is approximately 35% of the total cost of your wedding, you can save the most money by limiting your guest list.  If you hire a wedding consultant, s/he may be able to cut your cake and save you the cake-cutting fee.  Check this out with your facility or caterer. Reception sites that charge a room rental fee may waive this fee if you meet minimum requirements on food and beverages consumed. But try to negotiate this before you book the facility.

**Price Range:**  $300 - $1,000

## HORS D' OEUVRES

At receptions where a full meal is to be served, hors d' oeuvres may be offered to guests during the first hour of the reception. However, at a tea or cocktail reception, hors d' oeuvres will be the "main course."

**Options:**  There are many options for hors d' oeuvres, depending on the formality of your reception and the type of food to be served at the meal.  Popular items are foods that can easily be picked up and eaten with one hand.  Hors d' oeuvres may be set out on tables "buffet style" for guests to help themselves, or they may be passed around on trays by waiters and waitresses.

**Things To Consider:**  When selecting hors d' oeuvres for your reception, consider whether heating or refrigeration will be available and choose your food accordingly.  When planning your menu, consider the time of day.  You should select lighter hors d' oeuvres for a midday reception and heavier hors d' oeuvres for an evening reception.

**Tips To Save Money:**  Tray pass hors d'oeuvres during cocktail hour and serve a lighter meal.  Avoid serving hors d'oeuvres that are labor intensive or that require expensive ingredients.  Compare two or three caterers; there is a wide price range between caterers for the same food.  Compare the total cost of catering (main meal plus hors d'oeuvres) when selecting a caterer.  Consider serving hors d'oeuvres "buffet style."  Your guests will eat less this way than if waiters and waitresses are constantly serving them hors d'oeuvres.

**Price Range:**  $1 - $10/person

## MAIN MEAL / CATERER

If your reception is going to be in a hotel, restaurant or other facility that provides food, you will need to select a meal to serve your guests.   Most of these facilities will have a predetermined menu from which to select your meal.  If your reception is going to be in a facility that does not provide food, you will need to hire an outside caterer.   The caterer will be responsible for preparing, cooking, decorating and serving the food.

The caterer will also be responsible for beverages and for cleaning up after the event.   Before signing a contract, make sure you understand all the services the caterer will provide.   Your contract should state the amount and type of food and beverages that will be served, the way in which they will be served, the number of servers who will be available, the cost per item or person, and the rental items the caterer will provide such as tables, chairs and tableware.

**Options:**   Food can be served either buffet-style or as a sit-down meal. It should be chosen according to the time of day, year, and formality of the wedding.  Although there are many main dishes to choose from, chicken and beef are the most popular selections for a large event.  Ask your facility manager or caterer for their specialty. If you have a special type of food you would like to serve at your reception, select a facility or caterer who specializes in preparing it.

**Things To Consider:**   When hiring a caterer, check to see if the location for your reception provides refrigeration and cooking equipment.  If not, make sure your caterer is fully self supported with portable refrigeration and heating equipment.  A competent caterer will prepare much of the food in his/her own kitchen and should provide an adequate staff of cooks, servers, and bartenders. Ask for references and look at photos from previous parties so you know how the food will be presented; or better yet, visit an event they are catering.

**Questions To Ask:** Be sure to ask all the following questions before selecting a caterer:

What is the name and phone number of my contact person?
How many years have you been in business?
What percentage of your catering business is dedicated to wedding receptions?
Do you have liability insurance?
Are you licensed to serve alcohol?
What is your ratio of servers to guests?
How do your servers dress for wedding receptions?
What is your price range for a seated lunch?
What is your price range for a buffet lunch?
What is your price range for a seated dinner?
What is your price range for a buffet dinner?
How much gratuity is expected?
What is your labor fee per employee?
What is your cake-cutting fee?
What is your bartending fee?
What is your fee to clean-up after the reception?
What is your payment policy?
What is your cancellation policy?
Do you accept credit cards?
When is the final head-count needed?

**Beware:** Avoid mayonnaise, cream sauces, or custard fillings if food must go unrefrigerated for any length of time.

**Tips To Save Money:** Give only 85 to 95 percent of your final guest count to your caterer or facility manager, depending on how certain you are that all of your guests who have responded will come. Chances are that several, if not many, of your guests will not show up. If they do, your caterer should have enough food for all of them. This is especially true with buffet style receptions, in which case the facility or caterer will charge extra for each additional guest. However, if you give a complete count of your guests to your caterer and some of them don't show up, you will still have to pay for their plates. If offering a buffet meal, have the catering staff serve the food onto guests' plates rather than allowing guests to serve themselves. This will help to regulate the amount of food consumed.

Select food that is not too time-consuming to prepare, or food that does not have expensive ingredients. Also, consider a brunch or early afternoon wedding so the reception will fall between meals, allowing you to serve hors d'oeuvres instead of a full meal. Or tray pass hors d'oeuvres during cocktail hour and choose a lighter meal.

**Price Range:** $10 - $60/person

## LIQUOR / BEVERAGES

Prices for liquor and beverages vary greatly, depending on the amount and brand of alcohol served. It is an expected tradition that at least champagne or punch be served to toast the couple.

**Options:** White and red wines, scotch, vodka, gin, rum, and beer are the most popular alcoholic beverages. Sodas and fruit punch are popular nonalcoholic beverages served at receptions. And of course, don't forget coffee or tea. There are a number of options and variations for serving alcoholic beverages: a full open bar where you pay for your guests to drink as much as they wish; an open bar for the first hour, followed by a cash bar where guests pay for their own drinks; cash bar only; beer and wine only; nonalcoholic beverages only; or any combination thereof.

**Things To Consider:** If you're hosting an open bar at a facility that provides alcohol, ask the catering manager how they charge for liquor: by consumption or by number of bottles opened. Get this in writing and then ask for a full consumption report after the event.

If you plan to serve alcoholic beverages at a facility that does not provide liquor, make sure your caterer has a license to serve alcohol and that the facility allows alcoholic beverages. If you plan to order your own alcohol, do so three or four weeks before the event. If you plan to have a no-host or "cash" bar, consider notifying your guests so they know to bring cash with them. A simple line that says "No-Host Bar" on the reception card should suffice.

In selecting the type of alcohol to serve, consider the age and preference of your guests, the type of food that will be served, and the time of day your guests will be drinking.

On the average, you should allow 1 drink per person per hour at the reception. A bottle of champagne will usually serve six glasses. Never serve liquor without some type of food. Use the following chart to plan your beverage needs:

| Beverages | Amount based on 100 guests |
|---|---|
| Bourbon | 3 Fifths |
| Gin | 3 Fifths |
| Rum | 2 Fifths |
| Scotch | 4 Quarts |
| Vodka | 5 Quarts |
| White Wine | 2 Cases |
| Red Wine | 1 Case |
| Champagne | 3 Cases |
| Other | 2 Cases each: Club Soda, Seltzer Water, Tonic Water, Ginger Ale, Cola, Beer |

**Beware:**  In today's society, it is not uncommon for the hosts of a party to be held legally responsible for the conduct and safety of their guests. Keep this in mind when planning the quantity and type of beverages to serve. Also, be sure to remind your bartenders not to serve alcohol to minors.

**Tips To Save Money:**  To keep beverage costs down, serve punch, wine, or nonalcoholic drinks only. If your caterer allows it, consider buying liquor from a wholesaler who will let you return unopened bottles. Also, avoid salty foods such as potato chips, pretzels or ham. These foods will make your guests thirstier so they will tend to drink more.

Host alcoholic beverages for the first hour, then go to a cash bar. Or host beer, wine, and soft drinks only and have mixed drinks available on a cash basis. The bartending fee is often waived if you meet the minimum requirements on beverages consumed. For the toast, tray pass champagne only to those guests who want it, not to everyone. Many people will make a toast with whatever they are currently drinking. Consider serving sparkling cider in place of champagne.

Omit waiters and waitresses. Instead, have an open bar in which your guests have to get their own drinks. People tend to drink almost twice as much if there are waiters and waitresses constantly asking them if they would like another drink and then bringing drinks to them.

**Price Range:**  $8 - $25/person

## BARTENDING / BAR SET-UP FEE

Some reception sites and caterers charge an extra fee for bartending and for setting up the bar.

**Tips To Save Money:** The bartending fee could be and often is waived if you meet a minimum requirement on beverages consumed. Try to negotiate this with your caterer prior to hiring him/her.

**Price Range:** $50 - $375

## CORKAGE FEE

Many reception sites and caterers make money by marking up the food and alcohol they sell. You may wish to provide your own alcohol for several reasons. First, it is more cost effective. Second, you may want to serve an exotic wine or champagne that the reception site or caterer does not offer. In either case, and if your reception site or caterer allows it, be prepared to pay a corkage fee. This is the fee for each bottle brought into the reception and opened by a member of their staff.

**Things To Consider:** You need to consider whether the expenses saved after paying the corkage fee justify the hassle and liability of bringing in your own alcohol.

**Price Range:** $5 - $10/bottle

## FEE TO POUR COFFEE

In addition to the corkage and cake-cutting fees, some facilities also charge extra to pour coffee with the wedding cake.

**Things To Consider:**  Again, when comparing the cost of various reception sites, don't forget to add up all the extra miscellaneous costs, such as the fee for pouring coffee.

**Price Range:**  $0.25 - $0.75/person

## SERVICE PROVIDERS' MEALS

Service providers' meals are meals you serve your hired wedding professionals at the reception.

**Things To Consider:**  It is considered a courtesy to feed your photographer, videographer, and any other "service provider" at the reception.  Check options and prices with your caterer or reception site manager.  Make sure you allocate a place for your service providers to eat.  You may want them to eat with your guests, or you may prefer setting a place outside the main room for them to eat.  Your service providers may be more comfortable with the latter.

**Tips To Save Money:**  You don't need to feed your service providers the same meal as your guests.  You can order sandwiches or another less expensive meal for them.  If the meal is a buffet, there should be enough food left after all your guests have been served for your service providers to eat.  Tell them they are welcome to eat after all your guests have been served.  If this is the case, you may not be charged extra for your service providers to eat.  Be sure to discuss this with your catering manager.

**Price Range:**   $7 - $25/person

## GRATUITY

It is customary to pay a gratuity fee to your caterer. The average gratuity is 15% to 18% of your food and beverage bill.

**Tips To Save Money:** Gratuities can range from 15% to 25%. Ask about these costs up front and select your caterer or reception site accordingly.

**Price Range:** 15% - 18%

## PARTY FAVORS

Party favors are little gift items given to your guests as mementos of your wedding. They add a very special touch to your wedding and can become keepsakes for your guests.

**Options:** White matchboxes engraved with the couple's names; cocktail napkins marked in the same way; individually wrapped and marked chocolates, almonds, or fine candy are all popular party favors. Wine or champagne bottles marked with the bride and groom's names and wedding date on a personalized label are also very popular. These come in different sizes and can be purchased by the case.

If you can afford it, you may also consider porcelain or ceramic party favors. These can be custom-fired with your name and wedding date on them. A new idea that's gaining in popularity among environmentally conscientious couples is to present each guest with a tiny shoot of an endangered tree to be planted in honor of the bride and groom.

**Things To Consider:**    Personalized favors need to be ordered several weeks in advance.

**Price Range:**  $1 - $8/person

## DISPOSABLE CAMERAS

A great way to inexpensively obtain many candid photographs of your wedding day is to place a disposable 35 mm camera loaded with film on each table at your reception, and to have your guests take shots of the event!  Disposable cameras come pre-loaded with film.  Your guests can leave the cameras at their table or drop them in a basket or other labeled container near the entrance to the reception site.  Arrange for someone to collect the cameras after the event.  Tell your DJ, musician, or wedding coordinator to encourage your guests to take photographs with the disposables. You will end up with many beautiful, memorable and candid photographs of your reception.

**Things To Consider:**    Disposable cameras are sold with and without flash.  Disposable cameras with flash are more expensive but necessary if your reception is going to be held indoors or in the evening.  If you are planning a large reception, consider buying cameras with only 12 exposures.  Otherwise, you may end up with too many photographs.  For example, if 200 guests attend your reception and you seat 8 guests per table, you will need to purchase 25 cameras.  If each camera has 36 exposures, you will end up with 825 photographs.  If the cameras have only 12 exposures, you will end up with 300 photographs, which is a more reasonable quantity!

**Tips To Save Money:**  Instead of developing these photographs into print and then placing them into a big album, have your videographer transfer the negatives directly onto video set to your favorite music.  You can then reproduce this "photo montage" and send it as a gift to your friends and family members.  You can later decide which of these photographs you want to develop into print.

**Price Range:**   $4  - $13/camera

## ROSE PETALS / RICE

Rose petals or rice are traditionally tossed over the bride and groom as they leave the church after the ceremony or when they leave the reception.  These are usually handed out to guests in little sachet bags while the bride and groom are changing into their going away clothes.  This tradition was initiated in the Middle Ages whereby a handful of wheat was thrown over the bridal couple as a symbol of fertility.  Rose petals are used to symbolize happiness, beauty, and prosperity.

**Options:**  Rose petals, rice, or confetti is often used.  However, an environmentally correct alternative is to use grass or flower seeds, which do not need to be "cleaned up" if tossed over a grassy area.  These come wrapped in attractive, recycled packages with the couple's names and wedding date printed on the front.

**Things To Consider:**  Rose petals can stain carpets;  rice can sting faces, harm birds and make stairs dangerously slippery; confetti is messy and hard to clean.  Clubs and hotels seldom permit the use of any of these.  Ask about their policy.

**Price Range:**  $.35 - $1/person

## GIFT ATTENDANT

The gift attendant is responsible for watching over your gifts during the reception so that no one walks away with them.  This is necessary only if your reception is held in a public area such as a hotel or outside garden where other people may be walking by.  It is not proper to have a friend or family member take on this duty as s/he would not enjoy the reception.  The gift attendant should also be responsible for transporting your gifts from the reception to your car or bridal suite.

**Tips To Save Money:**  Hire a young boy or girl from your neighborhood to watch over your gifts at the reception.

**Price Range:**  $20 - $80

## PARKING FEE / VALET SERVICES

Many reception sites such as hotels, restaurants, etc.  charge for parking.  It is customary, although not necessary, for the host of the wedding to pay this charge.  At a large home reception, you should consider hiring a professional, qualified valet service if parking could be a problem.  If so, make sure the valet service is fully insured.

**Things To Consider:**  When comparing the cost of reception sites, don't forget to add the cost of parking to the total price.

**Tips To Save Money:**  To save money, let your guests pay their own parking fees.

**Price Range:**  $1.50 - $9/car

# Personal Notes

_____

_____

_____

_____

_____

_____

_____

_____

_____

_____

_____

_____

_____

_____

_____

_____

_____

_____

_____

_____

_____

USIC

## CEREMONY MUSIC

Ceremony music is the music played during the ceremony; i.e., prelude, processional, ceremony, recessional, and postlude. Prelude music is played 15 to 30 minutes before the ceremony begins and while guests are being seated. Processional music is played as the wedding party enters the ceremony site. Ceremony music is played during the ceremony. Recessional music is played as the wedding party leaves the ceremony site. Postlude music is played while guests leave the ceremony site.

**Options:** The most traditional musical instrument for wedding ceremonies is the organ. But guitars, pianos, flutes, harps and violins are also popular today. The two most popular musical selections for the processional are *Trumpet Voluntary* by Purcell and *The Bridal Chorus* by Wagner. Popular selections for the recessional are *Wedding March* by Mendelssohn and *Postlude in G Major* by Handel. *Canon in D Major* by Pachelbel and *Adagio in A Minor* by Bach are also popular selections for wedding ceremonies.

Popular musical selections for Jewish weddings are Erev Shel Shoshanim, Erev Ba, and Hana' Ava Babanot.

**Things To Consider:** Music may or may not be included as part of the ceremony site fee. Be sure to check with your ceremony site about restrictions pertaining to music and the availability of musical instruments for your use. Discuss the selection of ceremony music with your officiant and musicians. Make sure the musicians know how to play the selections you request.

When selecting ceremony music, keep in mind the formality of your wedding, your religious affiliation, and the length of the ceremony. Also consider the location and time of day. If the ceremony is outside where there may be other noises such as traffic, wind, or people's voices, or if a large number of guests will be attending your ceremony, consider having the music, your officiant, and your vows amplified. Make sure there are electrical outlets close to where the instruments will be set up.

**Questions To Ask:** Make sure you ask the following questions to ensure a smart hiring decision:

- What is the name and phone number of my contact person?
- How many years of professional experience do you have?
- What percentage of your business is dedicated to weddings?
- Are you the person who will perform at my wedding?
- What instrument(s) do you play?
- What type of music do you specialize in?
- What are your hourly fees?
- What is your cost for a soloist?
- What is your cost for a duet?
- What is your cost for a trio?
- What is your cost for a quartet?
- How would you dress for my wedding?
- Do you have liability insurance?
- Do you have a cordless microphone?
- What is your payment policy?
- What is your cancellation policy?

**Tips To Save Money:** Hire student musicians from your local university or high school. Ask a friend to sing or play at your ceremony; they will be honored.  If you're planning to hire a band for your reception, consider hiring a scaled-down version of the same band to play at your ceremony, such as a trio of flute, guitar, and vocals.  This could enable you to negotiate a "package" price.  If you're planning to hire a DJ for your reception, consider hiring him/her to play pre-recorded music at your ceremony.

**Price Range:**  $50 - $400

## RECEPTION MUSIC

Music is a major part of your reception, and should be planned carefully.  Music helps create the atmosphere of your wedding.  Special songs will make your reception unique.  When you select music for your reception, keep in mind the age and musical preference of your guests, your budget, and any restrictions that the reception site may have.  Bands and musicians are typically more expensive than DJ's.

**Options:**  There are many options for reception music:  you can hire a DJ, a band, an orchestra, or any combination of one or more instruments and vocalists.

**Things To Consider:**  Consider hiring an entertainment agency that can help you choose a reliable DJ or band that will play the type of music you want.  Whoever you choose should have experience performing at wedding receptions.

If you want your musician to act as a master of ceremonies, make sure s/he has a complete timeline for your reception so s/he knows when to announce the various events such as the toasts, first dance, and cutting of the cake.  Consider watching your musicians perform at another event before booking their services.

If you need a large variety of music to satisfy all your guests, consider hiring a DJ.  A professional DJ can play any type of music and may even offer a light show.  Make sure you give him/her a list of the songs you want played at your reception and a timeline for playing each one.  Make sure there are electrical outlets at the reception site close to where the musicians will be performing.

**Questions To Ask:**   Ask all the following questions to ensure a smart hiring decision:

- What is the name and phone number of my contact person?
- How many years of professional experience do you have?
- How many people are in your band?
- What percentage of your business is dedicated to wedding receptions?
- What type of music do you specialize in?
- What type of sound system do you have?
- Will you perform at my reception?
- Can you act as a master of ceremonies?
- How do you dress for receptions?
- Do you have a cordless microphone?
- Can you provide a light show?
- How many breaks do you take in a 4-hour reception?
- Do you play recorded music during breaks?
- How long are your breaks?
- Do you have liability insurance?
- What are your fees for a 4-hour reception?
- What is your cost per additional hour?
- What is your payment policy?
- What is your cancellation policy?

**Tips To Save Money:**  You will probably get a better price if you hire a band or DJ directly, rather than using an entertainment agency to hire your musicians.

Check the music department of local colleges and universities for names of student musicians and DJ's. You may be able to hire a student for a fraction of the price of a professional musician or DJ. A DJ is typically less expensive than a "live" musician, saving $200 - $1,000. Some facilities have contracts with certain DJ's, and you may be able to save money by hiring one of them.

**Price Range:**   $300 -$3,000

# Personal Notes

_____

_____

_____

_____

_____

_____

_____

_____

_____

_____

_____

_____

_____

_____

_____

_____

_____

_____

_____

_____

_____

_____

_____

_____

# *B*AKERY

## WEDDING CAKE

Wedding cakes may be ordered from a caterer or from a bakery. Some hotels and restaurants may also be able to provide a wedding cake. However, you will probably be better off ordering your cake from a bakery that specializes in wedding cakes. Ask to see photographs of other wedding cakes your baker has created, and by all means, ask for a tasting!

**Options:** When ordering your cake, you will have to decide not only on a flavor, but also on a size, shape and color. Size is determined by the number of guests. You can choose from one large tier to two, three, or more smaller tiers. The cake can be round, square or heart-shaped. The most common flavors are chocolate, carrot, lemon, rum, and "white" cakes. You can be creative by adding a filling to your cake, such as custard, strawberry, or chocolate. You may also want to consider having tiers of different flavors.

**Things To Consider:** Price, workmanship, quality, and taste vary considerably from baker to baker. In addition to flavor, size, and cost, consider decoration and spoilage (sugar keeps longer than cream frostings). The cake should be beautifully displayed on its own table decorated with flowers or greenery. Make sure the baker, caterer, or reception site manager can provide you with a pretty cake-cutting knife. If not, you will need to purchase or rent one.

When determining the size of the cake to order, don't forget that you'll be saving the top tier for your first anniversary. This top tier should be removed before the cake is cut and then wrapped in several layers of plastic wrap or placed in a sealed plastic container. It should be kept frozen until your anniversary.

**Questions To Ask:**   Be sure to ask all the following questions before selecting a bakery:

* What is the name and phone number of my contact person?
* How many years have you been making wedding cakes?
* What are your wedding cake specialties?
* Do you offer free tasting of your wedding cakes?
* Do you freeze your wedding cakes?
* How far in advance should I order my cake?
* Can you make a groom's cake?
* Do you lend, rent or sell cake knives?
* What is the cost per serving of my desired cake?
* What is your cake pillar and plate rental fee, if any?
* Is this fee refundable upon the return of these items?
* When must these items be returned?
* What is your cake delivery and set-up fee?
* What is your payment policy?
* What is your cancellation policy?

**Tips To Save Money:**   Compare taste, type and quality. Some bakers do not have set-up or delivery fees, some do. Check for individuals who bake from their home. They are usually more reasonable but you should check with the health department where you live. Some caterers have contracts with bakeries and can pass on savings to you. Some bakeries require a deposit on columns and plates. You lose the deposit if you fail to return these items to the baker within the specified time. Other bakeries use disposable columns and plates, saving you the rental fee and the hassle of returning these items.

**Price Range:**  $1 - $8/piece

## GROOM'S CAKE

The groom's cake is an old southern tradition whereby this cake is cut up and distributed to guests in little white boxes engraved with the bride and groom's names.  Today the groom's cake, if offered, is cut and served along with the wedding cake.

**Options:**  Usually a chocolate cake decorated with fruit.

**Tips To Save Money:**  Because of its cost and the labor involved in cutting and distributing the cake, very few people offer this delightful custom any more.

**Price Range:**  $0.75 - $1.50/piece

## CAKE DELIVERY & SET-UP FEE

This is the fee charged by bakers to deliver and set up your wedding cake at the reception site.  It usually includes a deposit on the cake pillars and plate which will be refunded upon their return to the baker.

**Tips To Save Money:**  Have a friend or family member get a quick lesson on how to set up your cake.  Have them pick it up and set it up the day of your wedding, then have the florist decorate the cake and/or cake table with flowers and greenery.

**Price Range:**  $20 - $50

## CAKE-CUTTING FEE

Most reception sites and caterers charge a fee for each slice of cake they cut if the cake is brought in from an outside bakery. This fee will probably shock you. It is simply their way of enticing you to order the cake through them. And unfortunately, many sites and caterers will not allow a member of your party to cut the cake.

**Tips To Save Money:**   Many hotels and restaurants include a dessert in the cost of their meal packages. If you forego this dessert and substitute your cake as the dessert, they may be willing to waive the cake-cutting fee. Be sure to ask them.

**Price Range:**  $.75 - 1.75/person

## CAKE TOP

The bride's cake is often topped and surrounded with fresh flowers, but traditional cake tops are also very popular.

**Options:**   Bells, love birds, a bridal couple or replica of two wedding rings are popular choices for cake tops and can be saved as mementos of your wedding day.

**Beware:**  Some porcelain and other heavier cake tops need to be anchored down into the cake. If you're planning to use a cake top other than flowers, be sure to discuss this with your baker.

**Tips To Save Money:**  Borrow a cake top from a friend or a family member as "something borrowed," an age-old wedding tradition. See "Wedding Traditions" on page 160.

**Price Range:**  $25 - $150

## CAKE  KNIFE / TOASTING GLASSES

Your cake knife and toasting glasses should compliment your overall setting; these items will bring you happy memories of your wedding day every time you use them.  The cake knife is used to cut the cake at the reception.  The bride usually cuts the first two slices of the wedding cake with the groom's hand placed over hers. The groom feeds the bride first, then the bride feeds the groom. This tradition makes beautiful wedding photographs.

You will need toasting glasses to toast each other after you cut the cake.  They are usually decorated with ribbons or flowers and kept near the cake.   This tradition also makes beautiful wedding photographs.

**Things To Consider:**  Consider having your initials and wedding date engraved on your wedding knife as a memento.  Consider purchasing crystal or silver toasting glasses as a keepsake of your wedding.  Have your florist decorate your knife and toasting glasses with flowers or ribbons.

**Tips To Save Money:**  Borrow your cake knife or toasting glasses from a friend or family member as "something borrowed," an age-old wedding tradition.  See "Wedding Traditions" on page 161. Use the reception facility's glasses and knife, and decorate them with flowers or ribbon.

**Price Range:**  $15 - $120/knife
               $30 - $80/toasting glasses

# Personal Notes

_____

_____

_____

_____

_____

_____

_____

_____

_____

_____

_____

_____

_____

_____

_____

_____

_____

_____

_____

_____

_____

_____

_____

_____

_____

# FLOWERS

## BRIDE'S BOUQUET

The bridal bouquet is one of the most important elements of the bride's attire and deserves special attention.  Start by selecting the color and shape of the bouquet.  Consider stephanotis -- tradition regards it as the bridal good-luck flower!  The bridal bouquet should be carried low enough so that all the intricate details of your gown are visible.

**Options:**   There are many colors, scents, sizes, shapes and styles of bouquets to choose from.  The traditional bridal bouquet is made of white flowers.  Stephanotis, gardenias, white roses, orchids and lilies of the valley are popular choices for an all-white bouquet.

If you prefer a colorful bouquet, you may want to consider using roses, tulips, stock, peonies, freesias, and Gerbera, which come in a wide variety of colors.  Using scented flowers in your bouquet will evoke memories of your wedding day whenever you smell them in the future.  Popular  fragrant flowers for bouquets are gardenias, freesias, magnolias, and wisteria.  Select flowers that are in season to assure availability.

### Popular Flowers for a Summer Bouquet:

| | | | |
|---|---|---|---|
| Allium | Amaryllis | Billy Buttons | Celosia |
| Dahlia | Delphinium | Liatris | Lisianthus |
| Pincushion | Queen Anne's Lace | | Saponaria |
| Sunflower | Snapdragon | Speedwell | Tuberose |

### Popular Flowers for a Fall Bouquet:

| | | | |
|---|---|---|---|
| Amaryllis | Anemones | Dahlia | Delphinium |
| Liatris | Lisianthus | Narcissus | Protea |
| Snapdragon | Star of Bethlehem | | Tuberose |

### Popular Flowers for a Winter Bouquet:

| | | | |
|---|---|---|---|
| Amaryllis | Anemone | Narcissus | |
| Protea | Star of Bethlehem | Tulip | Waxflower |

### Popular Flowers for a Spring Bouquet:

| | | | |
|---|---|---|---|
| Allium | Anemone | Billy Buttons | Celosia |
| Daffodils | Liatris | Lily of the Valley | |
| Lisianthus | Narcissus | Peony | Ranunculus |
| Snapdragon | Sunflower | Sweet Pea | Tulip |
| Waxflower | | | |

### Popular Flowers Year-Round:

| | | | |
|---|---|---|---|
| Alstroemeria | Aster | Baby's Breath | Bachelor's |
| Button | Bird of Paradise | Bouvardia | Calla Lily |
| Carnation | Chrysanthemum | Eucalyptus | Freesia |
| Gardenia | Gerbera | Gladiolus | Iris |
| Lily | Nerine | Orchid | Rose |
| Statice | Stephanotis | Stock | |

**Things To Consider:** Your flowers should complement the season, your gown, your color scheme, your attendants' attire, and the style and formality of your wedding.  If you have a favorite flower, build your bouquet around it and include it in all your arrangements.   Some flowers carry centuries of symbolism. Pimpernel signifies change; white flowers radiate innocence; forget-me-nots indicate true love;  and ivy stands for friendship, fidelity, and matrimony -- the three essentials for a happy marriage.

No flower, however, has as much symbolism for brides as the orange blossom, having at least 700 years of nuptial history.  Its unusual ability to simultaneously bear flowers and produce fruit symbolizes the fusion of beauty, personality, and fertility.

Whatever flowers you select, final arrangements should be made well in advance of your wedding date to insure availability. Confirm your final order and delivery time a few days before the wedding.   Have the flowers delivered before the photographer arrives so that you can include them in your pre-ceremony photos.

In determining the size of your bouquet, consider your gown and your overall stature.  Carry a smaller bouquet if you're petite or if your gown is fairly ornate.   A long, cascading bouquet complements a fairly simple gown or a tall or larger bride.  Arm bouquets look best when resting naturally in the crook of your arm.

For a natural, fresh-picked look, have your florist put together a cluster of flowers tied together with a ribbon.  For a Victorian appeal, carry a nosegay or a basket filled with flowers.  Or carry a Bible or other family heirloom decorated with just a few flowers. For a contemporary look, you may want to consider carrying an arrangement of calla lilies or other long-stemmed flower over your arm.  For a dramatic statement, carry a single stem of your favorite flower!

**Questions To Ask:** Be sure you ask all the following questions before selecting a florist:

- What is the name and phone number of my contact person?
- How many years of professional floral experience do you have?
- What percentage of your business is dedicated to weddings?
- Do you have access to out-of-season flowers?
- Will you visit the ceremony and reception sites to make floral recommendations?
- Can you preserve my bridal bouquet?
- Do you rent vases and candleholders?
- Can you provide silk flowers?
- What is your cost of a bridal bouquet made of a dozen white roses and stephanotis?
- What is your cost of a boutonniere made of a single white rose?
- What is your cost of a corsage made with two gardenias?
- Do you have liability insurance?
- What is your delivery and set-up fee?
- What is your payment policy?
- What is your cancellation policy?
- Do you accept credit cards?
- What are your hours?

**Beware:** If your bouquet includes delicate flowers that will not withstand hours of heat or a lack of water, make sure your florist uses a bouquet holder to keep them fresh. If you want to carry fresh-cut stems without a bouquet holder, make sure the flowers you select are hardy enough to go without water for the duration of your ceremony and reception.

**Tips To Save Money:** The cost of some flowers may be significantly higher during their off-season. So try to select flowers which are in bloom and plentiful at the time of your wedding. Avoid exotic, out-of-season flowers. Allow your florist to emphasize your colors using more reasonable, seasonal flowers to achieve your total look. If you have a favorite flower that is costly or out of season, consider using silk for that one flower.

Avoid scheduling your wedding on holidays such as Valentine's Day and Mother's Day when the price of flowers is higher. Because every attendant will carry or wear flowers, consider keeping the size of your wedding party down to accommodate your floral budget. Hire a florist who works from his/her home.

**Price Range:  -**  $60 - $500

## TOSSING BOUQUET

If you want to preserve your bridal bouquet, consider having your florist make a smaller, less expensive bouquet specifically for tossing. This will be the bouquet you toss to your single, female friends toward the end of the reception. Tradition has it that the woman who catches the bouquet is the next to be married. Have your florist include a few sprigs of fresh ivy in the tossing bouquet to symbolize friendship and fidelity.

**Tips To Save Money:** Use the floral cake top or guest book table "tickler bouquet" as the tossing bouquet. Or omit the tossing bouquet altogether and simply toss your bridal bouquet.

**Price Range:**  $10 - $30

## MAID OF HONOR'S BOUQUET

The maid of honor's bouquet can be somewhat larger or a different color than the rest of the bridesmaids' bouquets.
This will help to set her apart from the others.

**Price Range:**     $25 - $75

## BRIDESMAIDS' BOUQUETS

The bridesmaids' bouquets should complement the bridal bouquet but are generally smaller in size. The size and color should coordinate with the bridesmaids' dresses and the overall style of the wedding. Bridesmaids' bouquets are usually identical.

**Options:**     To personalize your bridesmaids' bouquets, insert a different flower in each of their bouquets to make a statement. For example, if one of your bridesmaids has been sad, give her a lily of the valley to symbolize the return of happiness. To tell a friend that you admire her, insert yellow jasmine. A pansy will let your friend know that you are thinking of her.

**Things To Consider:**   Choose a bouquet style (cascade, cluster, contemporary, hand-tied) that compliments the formality of your wedding and the height of your attendants. If your bridesmaids will be wearing floral print dresses, select flowers that complement the floral print.

**Tips To Save Money:**     Have your attendants carry a single stemmed rose, lily or other suitable flower for an elegant look that also saves money.

**Price Range:** $15 - $60

## MAID OF HONOR / BRIDESMAIDS' HAIRPIECE

For a garden-look, have your maid of honor and bridesmaids wear garlands of flowers in their hair. If so, provide your maid of honor with a slightly different color or variety of flower to set her apart from the others.

**Options:**    You may consider using artificial flowers for the hairpieces as long as they are in keeping with the flowers carried by members of the bridal party.   Since it is not always easy to find good artificial blooms, other types of hairpieces may be more satisfactory, durable, and attractive.

**Things To Consider:**  Flowers used for the hairpiece must be a sturdy and long-lived variety.

**Price Range:**  $8 - $25

## FLOWER GIRL'S HAIRPIECE

Flower girls often wear a wreath of flowers as a hairpiece.

**Options:**  This is another place where artificial flowers may be used, but they must be in keeping with the flowers carried by members of the bridal party.   Since it is not always easy to find good artificial blooms, other types of hairpieces may be more satisfactory, durable, and attractive.

**Things To Consider:**  If the flowers used for the hairpiece are not of a sturdy and long-lived  variety, a  ribbon,
bow, or hat might be a safer choice.

**Price Range:**  $8 - $25

## BRIDE'S GOING AWAY CORSAGE

You may want to consider wearing a corsage on your going-away outfit.  This makes for pretty photos as you and your new husband leave the reception for your honeymoon. Have your florist create a corsage which echoes the beauty of your bouquet.

**Beware:** Put a protective shield under lilies when using them as corsages, as their anthers will easily stain fabric. Be careful when using Alstroemeria as corsages, as its sap can be harmful if it enters the human bloodstream.

**Tips To Save Money:** Ask your florist if s/he can design your bridal bouquet in such a way that the center flowers may be removed and worn as a corsage. Or omit this corsage altogether.

**Price Range:** $10 - $25

## OTHER FAMILY MEMBERS' CORSAGES

The groom is responsible for providing flowers for his mother, the bride's mother, and the grandmothers. The officiant, if female, may also be given a corsage to reflect her important role in the ceremony. The corsages don't have to be identical, but they should be coordinated with the color of their dresses.

**Options:** The groom may order flowers that can be pinned to a pocketbook or worn around a wrist. He should ask which style the women prefer, and if a particular color is needed to coordinate with their dresses. Gardenias, camellias, white orchids, or Cymbidium orchids are excellent choices for corsages, as they go well with any outfit.

**Things To Consider:** The groom may also want to consider ordering corsages for other close family members, such as sisters and aunts. This will add a little to your floral expenses, but will make these female family members feel more included in your wedding and will let guests know that they are related to the bride and groom. Many women do not like to wear corsages, so the groom should check with them before ordering the flowers.

**Beware:** Put a protective shield under lilies when using them as corsages, as their anthers will easily stain fabric. Be careful when using Alstroemeria as corsages, as its sap can be harmful if it enters the human bloodstream.

**Tips To Save Money:** Ask your florist to recommend reasonable flowers for corsages. Dendrobium orchids are reasonable and make lovely corsages.

**Price Range:** $10 - $25

## GROOM'S BOUTONNIERE

The groom wears his boutonniere on the left lapel, nearest to his heart.

**Options:** Boutonnieres are generally a single blossom such as a rosebud, stephanotis, freesia or a miniature carnation. If a rosebud is used for the wedding party, have the groom wear two rosebuds, or add a sprig of baby's breath to differentiate him from the groomsmen.

**Things To Consider:** Consider using a small cluster of flowers instead of a single bloom for the groom's boutonniere.

**Beware:** Be careful when using Alstroemeria as a boutonniere, as its sap can be harmful if it enters the human bloodstream.

**Tips To Save Money:** Use mini-carnations rather than roses.

**Price Range:**    $4 - $10

## USHERS AND OTHER FAMILY MEMBERS' BOUTONNIERES

The groom gives each man in his wedding party a boutonniere to wear on his left lapel. The officiant, if male, may also be given a boutonniere to reflect his important role in the ceremony. The ring bearer may or may not wear a boutonniere, depending on his outfit. A boutonniere is more appropriate on a tuxedo than on knickers and knee socks.

**Options:**    Generally, a single blossom such as a rosebud, freesia, or miniature carnation is used as a boutonniere.

**Things To Consider:**    The groom should also consider ordering boutonnieres for other close family members such as fathers, grandfathers, and brothers. This will add a little to your floral expenses, but will make these male family members feel more included in your wedding and will let guests know that they are related to the bride and groom.

**Beware:**    Be careful when using Alstroemeria as boutonnieres, as its sap can be harmful if it enters the human bloodstream.

**Tips To Save Money:**    Use mini-carnations rather than roses.

**Price Range:**    $3 - $7

## MAIN ALTAR

The purpose of flowers at the main altar is to direct the guests' visual attention toward the front of the church or synagogue and to the bridal couple.  Therefore, they must be seen by guests seated in the back.  The flowers for the ceremony site can be as elaborate or as simple as you wish.  Your officiant's advice, or that of the altar guild or florist, can be most helpful in choosing flowers for the altar and chancel.

**Options:**  If your ceremony is outside, decorate the arch, gazebo, or other structure serving as the altar with flowers or greenery.  In a Jewish ceremony, vows are said under a Chuppah, which is placed at the altar and covered with greens and fresh flowers.

**Things To Consider:**  In choosing floral accents, consider the decor of your ceremony site.  Some churches and synagogues are ornate enough and don't need extra flowers.   Too many arrangements would get lost in the architectural splendor.  Select a few dramatic showpieces that will complement the existing decor.  Be sure to ask if there are any restrictions on flowers at the church or synagogue.  Remember, decorations should be determined by the size and style of the building, the formality of the wedding, the preferences of the bride, the cost, and the regulations of the particular site.

**Tips To Save Money:**  Decorate the ceremony site with greenery only.  Candlelight and greenery are elegant in and of themselves. Use greenery and flowers from your garden.  Have your ceremony outside in a beautiful garden or by the water, surrounded by nature's own splendor.

**Price Range:**  $50 - $1,000

## ALTAR CANDELABRA

In a candlelight ceremony, the candelabra may be decorated with flowers or greens for a dramatic effect.

**Options:**  Ivy may be twined around the candelabra, or flowers may be strung to them.

**Price Range:**  $25 - $50

## AISLE PEWS

Flowers, candles or ribbons are often used to mark the aisle pews and add color.

**Options:**  A cluster of flowers, a cascade of greens, or a cascade of flowers and ribbons are all popular choices for aisle pew decorations.  Candles with adorning greenery add an elegant touch.

**Things To Consider:**  Use hardy flowers that can tolerate being handled as pew ornaments.  Gardenias and camellias, for example, are too sensitive to last long.

**Beware:**  Avoid using Allium as aisle pew decorations as it has an odor of onions.

**Tips To Save Money:**  It is not necessary to decorate all of the aisle pews, if any at all.  To save money, decorate only the reserved family pews.  Or decorate every second or third pew.

**Price Range:**  $5 - $40

## RECEPTION SITE

Flowers add beauty, fragrance, and color to your reception. Flowers for the reception, like everything else, should fit your style and color scheme. Flowers can help transform a stark reception hall into a warm, inviting and colorful room.

**Options:** For an evening reception, use votive candles wherever possible to create a warm, romantic setting -- along walkways, around a pool, in bathrooms, etc. Use twinkle lights to achieve a magical effect. Place them on indoor or outdoor trees.

**Things To Consider:** Consider renting indoor plants or small trees to give your reception a garden-like atmosphere.

**Tips To Save Money:** You can save money by taking flowers from the ceremony to decorate the reception site. However, you must coordinate this move carefully to avoid having your guests arrive at an undecorated reception room. Use greenery to fill large areas. Trees and garlands of ivy can give a dramatic impact for little money. Use greenery and flowers from your garden. Have your reception outside in a beautiful garden or by the water, surrounded by nature's own beauty.

**Price Range:** $300 - $1,500

## HEAD TABLE

The head table is where the wedding party will sit during the reception. This important table should be decorated with a larger, more dramatic centerpiece than the guest tables.

**Things To Consider:** Consider using a different color or style of arrangement to set the head table apart from the other tables.

**Beware:**    Avoid using fragrant flowers, such as Allium or Narcissus, on tables where food is being served or eaten, as their fragrance may conflict with other aromas.

**Tips To Save Money:**    Decorate the head table with the bridal and attendants' bouquets.

**Price Range:**  $50 - $300

## GUEST TABLES

At a reception where guests are seated, a small flower arrangement may be placed on each table.

**Things To Consider:**  The arrangements should complement the table linens and the size of the table, and should be kept low enough so as not to hinder conversation among guests seated across from each other.

**Beware:**  Avoid using highly fragrant flowers on tables where food is being served or eaten.

**Tips To Save Money:**  To keep the cost down and for less formal receptions, use small potted flowering plants placed in white baskets, or consider using dried or silk arrangements that you can make yourself and give later as gifts.  Or place a wreath of greenery entwined with colored ribbon in the center of the table. Use a different colored ribbon at each table and assign your guests to tables by ribbon color  rather than by number.

**Price Range:**  $10 - $60

## BUFFET TABLE

If buffet tables are used, have some type of floral arrangement on the tables to add color and beauty to your display of food.

**Options:**   Whole fruits and bunches of berries offer a variety of design possibilities. Figs add a festive touch. Pineapples are a sign of hospitality.   Vegetables offer an endless array of options to decorate with.   Herbs are yet another option in decorating.   A mixture of rosemary and mint combined with scented geraniums makes a very unique table decoration.

**Things To Consider:**   Depending on the size of the table, place one or two arrangements at each side.

**Beware:**   Avoid placing carnations, snapdragons, and Star of Bethlehem next to buffet displays of fruits or vegetables, as these flowers are extremely sensitive to the gasses emitted by these foods.

**Price Range:**  $50 - $300

## PUNCH TABLE

Put an assortment of greens or a small arrangement of flowers at the punch table. See "Buffet Table" above.

**Price Range:**  $10 - $50

## CAKE TABLE

The wedding cake is often the central location at the reception. Decorate the cake table with flowers.

**Tips To Save Money:**  Have your bridesmaids place their bouquets on the cake table during the reception. Or decorate the cake top only and cover the base with greenery.

**Price Range:**  $15 - $25

## CAKE

Flowers are a beautiful addition to a wedding cake and are commonly seen spilling out between the cake tiers.

**Things To Consider:**   Use only nonpoisonous flowers, and have your florist - not the caterer - design the floral decorations for your cake.  A florist will be able to blend the cake decorations into your overall floral theme.

**Price Range:**  $20 - $60

## CAKE KNIFE

Decorate your cake knife with white ribbon and flowers.

**Things To Consider:**   Consider engraving the cake knife with your names and wedding date.

**Price Range:**   $5 - $20

## TOASTING GLASSES

Tie small flowers with white ribbons on the stems of your champagne glasses. These wedding accessories deserve a special floral touch since they will most likely be included in your special photographs.

**Things To Consider:**   Consider engraving your toasting glasses with your names and wedding date.

**Price Range:**   $10 - $30

## FLORAL DELIVERY & SET-UP

Most florists charge a fee to deliver flowers to the ceremony and reception sites and to arrange them on site.

**Things To Consider:**   Make sure your florist knows where your sites are and what time to arrive.

**Price Range:**   $25 - $100

# Personal Notes

_____

_____

_____

_____

_____

_____

_____

_____

_____

_____

_____

_____

_____

_____

_____

_____

_____

_____

_____

_____

_____

_____

_____

# *D*ECORATIONS

## TABLE CENTERPIECES

Each of the tables at your reception, including the head table, should be decorated with a centerpiece.

**Options:**   Candles, mirrors and flowers are popular choices for table centerpieces.   However, the options are endless.   Just be creative!  An arrangement of shells, for example, makes a very nice centerpiece for a seaside reception.  Votive candles set on top of a mirror make a romantic centerpiece for an evening reception.

A wreath of greenery woven with colored ribbon makes a delightful centerpiece.  Use a different color ribbon at each table and have your guests seated according to ribbon color!

**Things To Consider:**   Select a table centerpiece which complements your colors and/or setting.  The centerpiece for the head table should be larger or more elaborate than for the other tables.  Make sure that your centerpiece is kept low enough so as not to hinder conversation among guests seated across from each other.  Consider using a centerpiece that your guests can take home as a memento of your wedding.

**Tips To Save Money:**  Make your own table centerpieces using materials that are not expensive.

**Price Range:**  $5 - $30 each

## BALLOONS

Balloons are often used to decorate a reception site. A popular idea is to release balloons at the church or reception. This adds a festive, exciting, and memorable touch to your wedding. Balloons can be used to create an arch backdrop for the wedding cake or inexpensive centerpieces for the tables.

**Things To Consider:** Color coordinate your balloons to match your wedding color scheme. Choose colors from your bouquet or your bridesmaids' dresses. Balloons should be delivered and set up well in advance -- at least before the photographer shows up.

If you are planning to release balloons at the church or reception, check with your city. Releasing balloons in some cities might be illegal. Also make sure there are no wires in which balloons can get entangled. If they do, you could be held responsible for damages or cleanup expenses.

**Tips To Save Money:** Balloons are less expensive than fresh flowers and can be used as a substitute for flowers to decorate the reception site.

**Price Range:** $75 - $500

# TRANSPORTATION

## TRANSPORTATION

It is customary for the bride and her father to ride to the ceremony site together on the wedding day. You may also include some or all members of your wedding party. Normally a procession to the church begins with the bride's mother and several of the bride's attendants in the first vehicle. If desired, you can provide a second vehicle for the rest of the attendants. The bride and her father will go in the last vehicle. This vehicle will also be used to transport the bride and groom to the reception site after the ceremony.

**Options:** There are various options for transportation. The most popular choice is a limousine since it is big and open and can accommodate several people as well as your bridal gown. You can also choose to rent a car that symbolizes your personality as a couple.

There are luxury cars such as Mercedes Benz, sports cars such as a Ferraris, and vintage vehicles such as 1950's Thunderbirds or 1930's Cadillacs. If your ceremony and reception sites are fairly close together, and if weather permits, you might want to consider a more romantic form of transportation, such as a horse-drawn carriage.

**Things To Consider:** In some parts of the country, limousines are booked on a 3-hour minimum basis.

**Questions To Ask:** Make sure you ask all the following questions before selecting a transportation company:

* What is the name and phone number of my contact person?
* How many years have you been in business?
* How many vehicles do you have available?
* Can you provide a back-up vehicle in case of an emergency?
* What are the brand names of the vehicles available?
* What are the various sizes of vehicles available?
* How old are the vehicles?
* How many drivers are available?
* Can you show me photos of your drivers?
* How do your drivers dress for weddings?
* Do you have liability insurance?
* What is the minimum amount of time required to rent a vehicle?
* What is the cost per hour? Two hours? Three hours?
* How much gratuity is expected?
* What is your payment policy?
* What is your cancellation policy?

**Beware:** Make sure the company you choose is fully licensed and has liability insurance. Do not pay the full amount until after the event.

**Tips To Save Money:** Consider hiring only one large limousine. This limousine can transport you, your parents and your attendants to the ceremony, and then you and your new husband from the ceremony to the reception.

**Price Range:** $35 - $100/hour

# *R*ENTAL *I*TEMS

## BRIDAL SLIP RENTAL

The bridal slip is an undergarment which gives the bridal gown its proper shape.

**Things To Consider:**  Be sure to wear the same slip you'll be wearing on your wedding day during your fittings.  Many bridal salons rent slips.  Schedule an appointment to pick up your slip one week before the wedding; otherwise, there might not be one available on your wedding day.  If rented, the slip will have to be returned shortly after the wedding.   Arrange for someone to do this for you within the allotted time.

**Tips To Save Money:**  Rent a slip rather than purchasing one; chances are you will never use it again.

**Price Range:**  $15 - $45

## CEREMONY ACCESSORIES

Ceremony rental accessories are additional items needed for the ceremony but not included in the ceremony site fee.

**Options:**  Ceremony rental accessories may include the following items:

Aisle Runner:    A thin rug made of plastic, paper or cloth extending the length of the aisle. It is rolled out after the mothers are seated, just prior to the processional. Plastic or paper doesn't work well on grass; but if you must use one of these types of runners, make sure the grass is clipped short.

Kneeling Cushion: A small cushion or pillow placed in front of the altar where the bride and groom kneel for their wedding blessing.

Arch (Christian):    A white lattice or brass arch where the bride and groom exchange their vows, often decorated with flowers and greenery.

Chuppah (Jewish): A canopy under which a Jewish ceremony is performed, symbolizing cohabitation and consummation.

You may also need to consider renting audio equipment, aisle stanchions, candelabra, candles, candlelighters, chairs, heaters, a gift table, a guest book stand, and a canopy.

**Things To Consider:** If you plan to rent any accessories for your ceremony, make sure the rental supplier has been in business for a reasonable period of time and has a good reputation. Reserve the items you need well in advance. Find out the company's payment, reservation and cancellation policies.

Some companies allow you to reserve emergency items such as heaters or canopies without having to pay for them unless needed, in which case you would need to call the rental company a day or two in advance to request the items. If someone else requests the items you have reserved, the company should give you the right of first refusal.

**Questions To Ask:**   Make sure you ask the following questions before selecting a rental supplier for your ceremony or reception:

- What is the name and phone number of my contact person?
- How many years have you been in business?
- What are your hours of operation?
- Do you have liability insurance?
- What is the cost per item needed?
- What is the cost of pick-up and delivery?
- What is the cost of setting up the items rented?
- When would the items be delivered?
- When would the items be picked up after the event?
- What is your payment policy?
- What is your cancellation policy?

**Tips To Save Money:**   When considering a ceremony outside of a church, figure the cost of rental items.  Negotiate a package deal, if possible, by renting items for both the ceremony and the reception from the same supplier.  Consider renting these items from your florist so you only have to pay one delivery fee.

**Price Range:**  $100 - $400

## TENT / CANOPY

A large tent or canopy may be required for receptions held outdoors to protect you and your guests from the sun or rain. Usually rented through party rental suppliers, tents and canopies can be expensive due to the labor involved in delivery and set-up.

**Options:**   Tents and canopies come in different sizes and colors. Depending on the shape of your reception area, you may need to rent several smaller canopies rather than one large one.  Contact several party rental suppliers to discuss the options.

**Things To Consider:** Consider this cost when making a decision between an outdoor and an indoor reception. In cooler weather, heaters may also be necessary.

**Tips To Save Money:** Shop early and compare prices with several party rental suppliers.

**Price Range:**    $300 - $3,000

## DANCE FLOOR

A dance floor will be provided by most hotels and clubs. However, if your reception site does not have a dance floor, you may need to rent one through your caterer or a party rental supplier.

**Things To Consider:** When comparing prices of dance floors, include the delivery and set-up fees.

**Price Range:** $100 - $300

## TABLES / CHAIRS

You will have to provide tables and chairs for your guests if your reception site or caterer doesn't provide them as part of their package. For a full meal, you will have to provide tables and seating for all guests. For a cocktail reception, you only need to provide tables and chairs for approximately 30 to 50 percent of your guests. Ask your caterer or reception site manager for advice.

**Options:** There are various types of tables and chairs to choose from. The most common chairs for wedding receptions are white wooden or plastic chairs. The most common tables for receptions are round tables that seat 8 guests. The most common head table arrangement is several rectangular tables placed end-to-end to seat your entire wedding party on one side, facing your guests. Contact various party rental suppliers to find out what types of chairs and tables they carry as well as their price ranges.

**Things To Consider:**   When comparing prices of renting tables and chairs, include the cost of delivery and set-up.

**Tips To Save Money:** Attempt to negotiate free delivery and set-up with party rental suppliers in exchange for giving them your business.

**Price Range:**  $3 - $8/person

## LINEN / TABLEWARE

You will also need to provide linens and tableware for your reception if your reception site or caterer doesn't provide them as part of their package.

**Options:**   For a sit-down reception where the meal is served by waiters and waitresses, tables are usually set with a cloth (usually white, but may be color coordinated with the wedding), a centerpiece, and complete place settings. At a less formal buffet reception where guests serve themselves, tables are covered with a cloth but place settings are not mandatory. The necessary plates and silverware may be located at the buffet table, next to the food.

**Things To Consider:**   Linens and tableware depend on the formality of your reception. When comparing prices, include the cost of delivery and set-up.

**Price Range:**   $3 -$20/person

## HEATERS

You may need to rent heaters if your reception will be held outdoors and if the temperature may drop below sixty-five degrees.

**Options:**  There are electric and gas heaters, both of which come in different sizes.  Gas heaters are more popular since they do not have unsightly and unsafe electric cords.

**Price Range:**  $25 - $50

## LANTERNS

Lanterns are often used at evening receptions.

**Options:**  Many choices are available, from fire lanterns to electric ones.

**Things To Consider:**  Consider the formality of the reception and choose the proper lighting to complement your decorations.

**Price Range:**  $6 - $40/lamp

## OTHER RENTAL ITEMS  (TRASH CANS, ETC.)

If your reception site or caterer doesn't provide them, you will need to purchase, rent or borrow other miscellaneous items for your reception, such as trash cans, a gift table, trash bags, and so on.

# GIFTS

## BRIDE'S GIFT

The bride's gift is traditionally given by the groom to the bride. It is typically a personal gift such as a piece of jewelry.

**Options:**   A string of pearls, a watch, pearl earrings, or a gold chain with a heart-shaped charm holding photos of the two of you.

**Things To Consider:**   This gift is not necessary and should be given only if budget allows.

**Tips To Save Money:**   Consider omitting this gift. A pretty card from the groom proclaiming his eternal love for the bride is a very special yet inexpensive gift.

**Price Range:**   $50 - $500

## GROOM'S GIFT

The groom's gift is traditionally given by the bride to the groom.

**Options:**   A nice watch, an elegant pen set, or a dramatic photo of the bride framed in silver or crystal.

**Things To Consider:**   This gift is not necessary and should be given only if budget allows.

**Tips To Save Money:** Consider omitting this gift. A pretty card from the bride proclaiming her eternal love for the groom is a very special yet inexpensive gift.

**Price Range:** $50 - $500

## BRIDESMAIDS' GIFTS

Bridesmaids' gifts are given by the bride to her bridesmaids and maid of honor as a permanent keepsake of the wedding.

**Options:** For bridesmaids' gifts, consider items of jewelry that can be worn both during and after the wedding; silver or crystal frames; or small handbags that the bridesmaids can carry to the wedding, filled with wedding day essentials such as lipstick, nail polish, jewelry, and pantyhose.

**Things To Consider:** Bridesmaids' gifts are usually presented at the bridesmaids' luncheon, if there is one, or at the rehearsal dinner. The gift to the maid of honor may be similar to the bridesmaids' gifts but should be a bit more expensive.

**Tips To Save Money:** Ask your photographer to take, at no extra charge, professional portraits of each bridesmaid and her escort for use as bridesmaids' gifts. Select a beautiful background that will remind your bridesmaids of the occasion, such as your cake table. Put the photo in a pretty frame. This makes a very special yet inexpensive gift for your attendants.

**Price Range:** $25 - $100/gift

## USHERS' GIFTS

Ushers' gifts are given by the groom to his ushers as a permanent keepsake of the wedding.

**Options:**  For ushers' gifts, consider fancy pen sets, wallets, leather belts, silver frames, watches, and desk clocks.

**Things To Consider:**  The groom should deliver his gifts to the ushers at the bachelor party or at the rehearsal dinner.  The gift to the best man may be similar to the ushers' gifts but should be a bit more expensive.

**Tips To Save Money:**  Negotiate with your photographer to take, at no extra charge, professional portraits of each usher and his escort for use as ushers' gifts.  Select a beautiful background that will remind your ushers of the occasion, such as your cake table. This makes a  special yet inexpensive gift for your attendants.

**Price Range:**  $25 - $100/gift

# PERSONAL NOTES

_____
_____
_____
_____
_____
_____
_____
_____
_____
_____
_____
_____
_____
_____
_____
_____
_____
_____
_____
_____
_____

# $\mathcal{P}$ARTIES

## BRIDESMAIDS' LUNCHEON

The bridesmaids' luncheon is given by the bride for her bridesmaids. It is not a shower; rather, it is simply a time for good friends to get together formally before the bride changes her status from single to married.

**Things To Consider:** You can give your bridesmaids their gifts at this gathering. Otherwise, plan to give them their gifts at the rehearsal dinner.

**Price Range:** $12 - $30/meal

## REHEARSAL DINNER

It is customary that the groom's parents host a dinner party following the rehearsal, the evening before the wedding. The dinner usually includes the bridal party, their spouses or guests, both sets of parents, close family members, the officiant, and the wedding consultant and/or coordinator.

**Options:** The rehearsal dinner party can be held just about anywhere, from a restaurant, hotel, or private hall to the groom's parents' home. Close relatives and out-of- town guests may be included if budget permits.

**Tips To Save Money:**  Restaurants specializing in Mexican food or pizza are fun yet inexpensive options for a casual rehearsal dinner.

**Price Range:**  $10 - $30/person

# *M*ISCELLANEOUS

## NEWSPAPER ANNOUNCEMENTS

There are two types of announcements you can send to your local newspaper:   one to announce your engagement, and one to announce your wedding.

For your engagement announcement, send information to the newspapers, along with a photograph, right after your engagement or at least 4 to 6 weeks before the wedding.  The photograph is usually the head and shoulders of the engaged couple.  The photograph should be wallet-sized or larger, black and white, and glossy.  Call your local newspapers to ask about their requirements.  Most papers will not take orders over the phone, so you will need to mail the information or deliver it personally.

For your wedding announcement, send information to the newspapers, along with a photograph of either the bride alone or the bridal couple, at least three weeks before the wedding.  The photograph should be wallet-sized or larger, black and white, and glossy.  Your photograph should show the way you will look the day of your wedding.  The announcement should appear the day following the ceremony.

**Things To Consider:**  If you and your fiancé grew up in different towns, consider sending announcements to the local papers of both towns.  If either of you is having second thoughts about the wedding, cancel both announcements as soon as possible.

**Tips To Save Money:** If you don't mind having your wedding announced a few weeks after the wedding, you can send a photo from your actual wedding day. This will save you the cost and hassle of dressing up to have your photo taken before the wedding.

**Price Range:** $40 - $80 (depending on size)


## MARRIAGE LICENSE

Marriage license requirements are state-regulated and may be obtained from the County Clerk in most county courthouses.

**Options:** Some states (California and Nevada, for example) offer two types of marriage licenses: a public license and a confidential one. The public license is the most common one and requires a health certificate and a blood test. It can only be obtained at the County Clerk's office.

The confidential license is usually less expensive and does not require a health certificate or blood test. If offered, it can usually be obtained from most Justices of the Peace. An oath must be taken in order to receive either license.

**Things To Consider:** Requirements vary from state to state but generally include the following points:

1. Applying for and paying the fee for the marriage license. There is usually a waiting period before the license is valid and a limited time before it expires.

2. Meeting residency requirements for the state and/or county where the ceremony will take place.

3.  Meeting the legal age requirements for both bride and groom or having parental consent.

4.  Presenting any required identification, birth or baptismal certificates, marriage eligibility or other documents.

5.  Obtaining a medical examination and/or blood test for both the bride and groom to detect communicable diseases.

**Price Range:**  $20 - $85

## PRENUPTIAL AGREEMENT

A prenuptial agreement is a legal contract between the bride and groom itemizing the property each brings into the marriage and explaining how those properties will be divided in case of divorce or death.  Although you can write your own agreement, it is advisable to have an attorney draw up or review the document. The two of you should be represented by different attorneys.

**Things To Consider:**   Consider a prenuptial agreement if one or both of you have a significant amount of capital or assets, or if there are children involved from a previous marriage.  If you are going to live in a different state after the wedding, consider having an attorney from that state draw up or review your document.

Nobody likes to talk about divorce or death when planning a wedding, but it is very important to give these issues your utmost consideration.  By drawing a prenuptial agreement, you encourage open communication and get a better idea of each other's needs and expectations.  You should also consider drawing up or reviewing your wills at this time.

**Tips To Save Money:**　Some software packages allow you to write your own will and prenuptial agreement, which can save you substantial attorney's fees.　However, if you decide to draw either agreement on your own, you should still have an attorney review it.

**Price Range:**　$500 - $3,000

## BRIDAL GOWN PRESERVATION

The pride and joy you will experience in seeing your daughter and/or granddaughter wear your wedding gown on her wedding day will more than justify the expense of having your gown preserved.　Bring your gown to a reputable dry cleaning company which specializes in preserving wedding gowns.　They will dry clean your dress, vacuum seal it, and place it in an attractive box. By doing this, your gown will be protected from yellowing, falling apart, or getting damaged over the years.　Most boxes have a plastic see-through window where you can show the top part of your dress to friends and family members without having to open the vacuum-sealed container.

**Tips To Save Money:**　Some bridal boutiques offer gown preservation.　Try to negotiate having your gown preserved for free with the purchase of a wedding gown.　It's well worth the try!　But remember, get any agreement in writing and be sure to have it signed by either the owner or the manager of the boutique.

**Price Range:**　$100 - $200

## BRIDAL BOUQUET PRESERVATION

The bridal bouquet can be preserved to make a beautiful memento of the wedding.

**Things To Consider:**   Have your bouquet dried, mounted, and framed to hang on your wall or to display on an easel in a quiet corner of your home.   You can also have an artist paint your bouquet.

**Price Range:** $100 - $500

## WEDDING CONSULTANT

Wedding consultants are professionals whose training, expertise, and contacts will help make your wedding as close to perfect as it can possibly be.  They can save you considerable time, money and stress when planning your wedding. Wedding consultants have information on many ceremony and reception sites as well as reliable service providers such as photographers, videographers and florists, which will save you hours of investigation and legwork.

Wedding consultants can provide facilities and service providers to match your budget.  They can also save you stress by ensuring that what you are planning is correct and that the service providers you hire are reliable and professional.   Most service providers recommended by wedding consultants will go out of their way to do an excellent job for you so that the wedding consultant will continue to recommend their services.

**Options:**  You can have a wedding consultant help you do as much or as little as you think necessary.  A consultant can help you plan the whole event from the beginning to the end, helping you formulate a budget and select your ceremony and reception sites, flowers, wedding gown, invitations, and service providers; or s/he can help you at the end by coordinating the rehearsal and the wedding day.  Remember, you want to feel like a guest at your own wedding.  You and your family should not have to worry about any details on that special day.

**Things To Consider:** Strongly consider engaging the services of a wedding consultant. Contrary to what many people believe, a wedding consultant is part of your wedding budget, not an extra expense! A good wedding consultant should be able to save you at least the amount of his/her fee by suggesting less expensive alternatives that still enhance your wedding. In addition, many consultants obtain discounts from the service providers they work with. If this is not enough, they are more than worth their fee by serving as an intermediary between you and your parents and/or service providers.

When hiring a wedding consultant, make sure you check his/her references. Ask the consultant if s/he is a member of the Association of Bridal Consultants (ABC) and ask to see a current membership certificate. All ABC members agree to uphold a Code of Ethics and Standards of Membership. Many consultants have formal training and experience in event planning and in other specialties related to weddings, such as flower arranging and catering.

**Questions To Ask:** Be sure you ask all the following questions to ensure a smart hiring decision:

- How many years of professional experience do you have?
- How many consultants are in your company?
- Are you a member of the Association of Bridal Consultants?
- What services do you provide?
- What are your hourly fees?
- What is your fee for complete wedding planning?
- What is your fee for the rehearsal and wedding day?
- What is your payment policy?
- What is your cancellation policy?
- Do you have liability insurance?

**Price Range:** $400 - $3,000

## WEDDING PLANNING SOFTWARE

With a computer, you can ease the process of planning your wedding. A good wedding planning software will help you create a budget, generate a guest list, address invitations, create a wedding timeline or schedule of events, keep track of payments made to service providers, and keep track of invitations sent as well as RSVPs and gifts received.

**Options:** One of the best wedding planning software programs available is published by Wedding Solutions Publishing, Inc. and is called *Easy Wedding Planning Software for Windows*. This software is very easy to use and will greatly help you plan all aspects of your wedding. The basic software package is included in this book. The User's Manual can be found on page 199.

**Price Range:** $30 - $60

## TAXES

Don't forget to figure-in the cost of taxes on all taxable items you purchase for your wedding. Many people make a big mistake by not figuring out the taxes they will have to pay for their wedding expenses. For example, if you are planning a reception for 250 guests with an estimated cost of $60/person for food and beverages, your pretax expenses would be $15,000. A sales tax of 7.5% would mean an additional expense of $1,125! Find out what the sales tax is in your area and which items are taxable, and figure this expense into your overall budget.

# Personal Notes

_____

_____

_____

_____

_____

_____

_____

_____

_____

_____

_____

_____

_____

_____

_____

_____

_____

_____

_____

_____

# WEDDING TRADITIONS

Have you ever wondered why certain things are almost always done at weddings? For example, why the bride carries a bouquet or wears a veil? Or why guests throw rice or rose petals over the newlyweds? Everything has a reason. In this section we discuss the origin and symbolism of some of the most popular wedding traditions.

This comprehensive list of wedding traditions comes from a delightful little book entitled *The Romance of the Wedding Ceremony* by Rev. Richleigh Hale Powers, Ph.D. This book has helped many couples personalize their wedding ceremony in a format that is both fun and easy to use.

## THE BRIDE'S BOUQUET

Bridal bouquets have evolved through the ages. Saracen brides carried bouquets of orange blossoms to symbolize fertility, and Roman brides carried sheaves of wheat to symbolize prosperity for their husbands. In the eighteenth century, the practice of carrying a bouquet of flowers or herbs became a popular tradition which symbolized fragility, purity, and new life. Bouquets of dill were among the most popular herb carried. After the ceremony the dill was eaten to "provoke lust." Today bridal bouquets are tossed to assembled single women to symbolize new life and to pass on the bride's good fortune.

## THE SPECIAL MEANING OF THE BRIDE'S VEIL

The veil represents modesty and respect. It symbolizes the sanctity and exclusiveness of the marriage covenant and reminds the couple and the witnesses that the physical relationship is to be entered into only after the vows are completed.

## RICE AND PETALS

In the Middle Ages, handfuls of wheat were thrown over married couples to symbolize the hope for fertility. In modern times, rice is typically thrown as it also symbolizes fertility. In recent years, flower petals have become another alternative, symbolizing beauty, happiness and prosperity.

## "SOMETHING OLD, SOMETHING NEW, SOMETHING BORROWED, SOMETHING BLUE"

Old and new items jointly symbolize the passage from the old unmarried state to that of the new married union. The wearing of a borrowed belonging demonstrates community participation in and approval of the wedding. Blue is worn because it is the color that signifies purity, love, and fidelity.

## WHITE AISLE RUNNER

A white aisle runner symbolizes walking on holy ground. A marriage covenant is not made merely between two people and their witnesses. It is made in the presence of God and He is actively involved in the agreement. The white aisle runner symbolizes God's holiness.

## SPECIAL SEATING FOR THE PARENTS

The parents of the bride and groom are part of the marriage covenant. The commitments they make during the ceremony are just as binding as the vows of the couple. The final responsibility of parents for their children is to determine with them God's will for a life partner. Thereafter, they serve in a chain of counsel for them and their children. Parents enter in the line of authority and leave in the line of counsel.

## THE GROOM ENTERING FIRST

By this action the groom signifies that he is the covenant initiator. This is important because whoever initiates the covenant assumes greater responsibility for seeing it fulfilled.

## THE FATHER OF THE BRIDE WALKING DOWN THE AISLE

This action has two meanings. By doing so, the father is saying to the bride, "I am endorsing this young man as God's very best choice of a husband for you, and I am now bringing you to him." In addition, the father is saying to the young man, "I am presenting to you a daughter who I have earnestly endeavored to raise as a pure bride."

## THE BRIDE AND GROOM TAKING EACH OTHER'S RIGHT HAND DURING THE CEREMONY

The open right hand offered by each party symbolizes their strength, resources and purpose. By clasping each other's right hand, they pledge these qualities to each other so that each partner can depend on all the resources that the other brings into the covenant relationship.  The handclasp goes far beyond sealing the contract.  It symbolizes the cleaving together of lives which is to be accomplished in the marriage covenant.

## THE GROOM MAKING THE FIRST VOW

The groom must be the leader and assume greater responsibility to fulfill the marriage covenant.  As covenant initiator, he must commit himself to the purposes of marriage which God established in the beginning.  And these must be reflected in his vows.

## THE SYMBOLISM OF THE WEDDING RINGS

The wedding rings symbolize the promises binding two people together in marriage.  The unbroken circle of the wedding band represents the continuity of undying love.  Greek theory believed the fourth finger of the left hand to be connected to the heart, making this the appropriate finger to be "bound" in romantic attachment.

## KISSING THE BRIDE

During the Roman empire, the kiss symbolized a legal bond. Continued use of the kiss to seal the marriage bond is based on the deeply rooted idea of the kiss as a vehicle for transference of power and souls.

## THE COUPLE BEING PRONOUNCED "HUSBAND AND WIFE"

This establishes their change of names and a definite point in time for the beginning of the marriage.  These words are to remove any doubt in the minds of the couple or the witnesses concerning the validity of the marriage.

## SIGNING THE WEDDING PAPERS

The newlyweds sign the wedding papers to establish a public document and public record of the covenant.

## SIGNING THE GUEST BOOK

Your wedding guests are official witnesses to the covenant. By signing the guest book, they are saying, "I have witnessed the vows, and I will testify to the reality of this marriage." Because of this significance, the guest book should be signed after the wedding rather than before it.

## THE PURPOSE OF THE RECEIVING LINE

The receiving line is for guests to give their blessings to the couple and their parents.

## THE MEANING OF SERVING FOOD AT THE RECEPTION

Food is part of the covenant celebration. It further symbolizes the unity of the couple. Entering into a meal itself is a form of covenant.

## THE BRIDE AND GROOM FEEDING WEDDING CAKE TO EACH OTHER

This represents the sharing of their body to become one. A New Testament illustration of this symbolism is The Lord's Supper.

# PERSONAL NOTES

_____

_____

_____

_____

_____

_____

_____

_____

_____

_____

_____

_____

_____

_____

_____

_____

_____

_____

_____

_____

_____

# *D*O'S & *D*ON'TS

Your wedding will last only a few hours but will likely take several months to plan. That is why it is so important to enjoy the complete wedding planning process. This is a time to get excited, to fall even more deeply in love with each other, to learn more about each other and how to give and take. If you can handle your wedding planning with your fiancé and parents, you can handle anything! Here is a list of do's and don'ts when planning your special day. If you follow these suggestions, your wedding planning and your wedding day will be more enjoyable!

## DO'S

Read this book completely.

Hire a professional wedding consultant.

Maintain a sense of humor.

Maintain open communication with your fiancé and with both sets of parents, especially if they are financing the wedding.

Be receptive to your parents' ideas, especially if they are financing the wedding.

Be flexible and keep your overall budget in mind.

Maintain a regular routine of exercise and eat a well-balanced diet.

Buy the *Indispensable Groom's Guide,* published by Wedding Solutions Publishing, Inc., and give it to your fiancé.

Buy the *Wedding Party Responsibility Cards,* published by Wedding Solutions Publishing, Inc., and give a card to each member of your wedding party.

Register for gifts;   consider a price range that your guests can afford.

Break-in your shoes well before your wedding day.

Practice with makeup and various hairstyles for your wedding day.

Check recent references for all of your service providers.

Get everything in writing with your service providers.

Assign your guests to tables and group them together by age, interests, acquaintances, etc.

Consider drawing-up a prenuptial agreement and a will.

Send thank-you notes as soon as you receive gifts.
Give a rose to each of your mothers as you walk down the aisle during the recessional.

Try to spend some time with each of your guests and personally thank them for coming to your wedding.

Encourage the bride's parents to introduce their family and friends to the family and friends of the groom's family, and vice-versa.

Toast both sets of parents at the rehearsal dinner and/or at the reception. Thank them for everything they have done for you and for giving you a beautiful wedding.

Eat well at the reception, especially if you will be drinking alcohol.

Keep a smile on your face; there will be many photographs taken of both of you.

Expect things to go wrong on your wedding day. Most likely something will go wrong, and no one will notice it but yourself. Relax and don't let it bother you.

Preserve the top tier of your wedding cake for your first year anniversary.

Send a special gift to both sets of parents, such as a small album containing the best photographs of the wedding. Personalize this gift by having it engraved with your names and the date of your wedding.

## DON'TS

Don't get involved in other activities; you will be very busy planning your wedding.

Don't make any major decisions without discussing it openly with your fiancé.

Don't be controlling. Be open to other people's ideas.

Don't overspend your budget; this can be extremely stressful.

Don't wait until the last minute to hire your service providers. The good ones get booked months in advance.

Don't try to make everyone happy; it is impossible and will only make your wedding planning more difficult.

Don't try to impress your friends.

Don't invite old boyfriends or girlfriends to your wedding; you don't want to make anybody uncomfortable.

Don't try to do "everything." Delegate responsibilities to your fiancé, your parents, and to members of your wedding party.

Don't rely on friends or family to photograph or videotape your wedding. Hire professionals!

Don't assume that members of your wedding party know what to do. Give them direction with the *Wedding Party Responsibility Cards*, available at most major bookstores and from Wedding Solutions Publishing, Inc. (see Order Form on page 259).

Don't assume your service providers know what to do.

Don't schedule your bachelor party the night before the wedding. You don't want to have a hangover on your special day!

Don't arrive late at the ceremony!

Don't get drunk during your reception; you don't want to make a fool of yourself on your most special day.

Don't flirt with members of the opposite sex.

Don't allow your guests to drive drunk after the reception; you may be held responsible.

Don't rub cake in the face of your spouse during the cake-cutting ceremony; your spouse might not appreciate it!

Don't overeat; this may upset your stomach or make you sleepy.

Don't leave your reception without saying good-bye to your family and friends.

Don't drive if you have had too much to drink.

# Personal Notes

_____

_____

_____

_____

_____

_____

_____

_____

_____

_____

_____

_____

_____

_____

_____

_____

_____

_____

_____

_____

_____

_____

# WEDDING PARTY

# RESPONSIBILITIES

Each member of your wedding party has his/her own individual duties and responsibilities. The following is a list of the most important duties for each member of your wedding party.

The most convenient method for conveying this information to members of your wedding party is by purchasing a set of the *Wedding Party Responsibility Cards,* published by Wedding Solutions Publishing, Inc.

These cards are very attractive and contain all the information your wedding party needs to know to assure a smooth wedding; i.e., what to do, how to do it, when to do it, when to arrive, and much more. They also include financial responsibilities as well as the processional, recessional and altar line-ups.

These cards are available at most major bookstores. You can also order them directly through Wedding Solutions Publishing, Inc. by filling out the Order Form on page 259.

# Maid of Honor

- Helps bride select attire and address invitations.
- Plans bridal shower for bride.
- Arrives at dressing site 2 hours before ceremony to assist bride in dressing.
- Arrives dressed at ceremony site 1 hour before the wedding for photographs.
- Arranges the bride's veil and train before the processional and recessional.
- Holds bride's bouquet and groom's ring, if no ring bearer, during the ceremony.
- Witnesses the signing of the marriage license.
- Keeps bride on schedule.
- Dances with best man during the bridal party dance.
- Helps bride change into her going away clothes.
- Mails wedding announcements after the wedding.
- Returns bridal slip, if rented.

# BEST MAN

- Responsible for organizing ushers' activities.
- Organizes bachelor party for groom.
- Drives groom to ceremony site and sees that he is properly dressed before the wedding.
- Arrives dressed at ceremony site 1 hour before the wedding for photographs.
- Brings marriage license to wedding.
- Pays the clergyman, musicians, photographer, and any other service providers the day of the wedding.
- Holds the bride's ring for the groom, if no ring bearer, until needed by officiant.
- Witnesses the signing of the marriage license.
- Drives newlyweds to reception if no hired driver.
- Offers first toast at reception, usually before dinner.
- Keeps groom on schedule.
- Dances with maid of honor during the bridal party dance.
- May drive couple to airport or honeymoon suite.
- Oversees return of tuxedo rentals for groom and ushers, on time and in good condition.

# *B*RIDESMAIDS

- Assist maid/matron of honor in planning bridal shower.
- Assist bride with errands and addressing invitations.
- Participate in all pre-wedding parties.
- Arrive at dressing site 2 hours before ceremony.
- Arrive dressed at ceremony site 1 hour before the wedding for photographs.
- Walk behind ushers in order of height during the processional, either in pairs or in single file.
- Sit next to ushers at the head table.
- Dance with ushers and other important guests.
- Encourage single women to participate in the bouquet-tossing ceremony.

# *U*SHERS

- Help best man with bachelor party.
- Arrive dressed at ceremony site 1 hour before the wedding for photographs.
- Distribute wedding programs and maps to the reception as guests arrive.
- Seat guests at the ceremony as follows:
  -- If female, offer the right arm.
  -- If male, walk along his left side.
  -- If couple, offer right arm to female; male follows a step or two behind.
  -- Seat bride's guests in left pews.
  -- Seat groom's guests in right pews.
  -- Maintain equal number of guests in left and right pews, if possible.
  -- Should a group of guests arrive at the same time, seat the eldest woman first.
  -- Just prior to the processional, escort groom's mother to her seat; then escort bride's mother to her seat.
- Two ushers may roll carpet down the aisle after both mothers are seated.
- If pew ribbons are used, two ushers may loosen them one row at a time after the ceremony.
- Direct guests to the reception site.
- Dance with bridesmaids and other important guests.

# BRIDE'S MOTHER

- Helps prepare guest list for bride and her family.
- Helps plan the wedding ceremony and reception.
- Helps bride select her bridal gown.
- Helps bride keep track of gifts received.
- Selects her own attire according to the formality and color of the wedding.
- Makes accommodations for bride's out of town guests.
- Arrives dressed at ceremony site 1 hour before the wedding for photographs.
- Is the last person to be seated right before the processional begins.
- Sits in the left front pew to the left of bride's father during the ceremony.
- May stand up to signal the start of the processional.
- Can witness the signing of the marriage license.
- Dances with the groom after the first dance.
- Acts as hostess at the reception.

# BRIDE'S FATHER

- Helps prepare guest list for bride and her family.
- Selects attire that complements groom's attire.
- Rides to the ceremony with bride in limousine.
- Arrives dressed at ceremony site 1 hour before the wedding for photographs.
- After giving bride away, sits in the left front pew to the right of bride's mother.  If divorced, sits in second or third row unless financing the wedding.
- When officiant asks, "Who gives this bride away?" answers, "Her mother and I do" or something similar.
- Can witness the signing of the marriage license.
- Dances with bride after first dance.
- Acts as host at the reception.

# GROOM'S MOTHER

- Helps prepare guest list for groom and his family.
- Selects attire that complements mother of the bride's attire.
- Makes accommodations for groom's out-of-town guests.
- With groom's father, plans rehearsal dinner.
- Arrives dressed at ceremony site 1 hour before the wedding for photographs.
- May stand up to signal the start of the processional.
- Can witness the signing of the marriage license.

# GROOM'S FATHER

- Helps prepare guest list for groom and his family.
- Selects attire that complements groom's attire.
- With groom's mother, plans rehearsal dinner.
- Offers toast to bride at rehearsal dinner.
- Arrives dressed at ceremony site 1 hour before the wedding for photographs.
- Can witness the signing of the marriage license.

# *F*LOWER *G*IRL

- Usually between the ages of four and eight.
- Attends rehearsal to practice her role but is not required to attend pre-wedding parties.
- Arrives dressed at ceremony site 45 minutes before the wedding for photographs.
- Carries a basket filled with loose rose petals to strew along bride's path during processional, if allowed by ceremony site.
- If very young, may sit with her parents during ceremony.

# *R*ING *B*EARER

- Usually between the ages of four and eight.
- Attends rehearsal to practice his role but is not required to attend pre-wedding parties.
- Arrives at ceremony site 45 minutes before the wedding for photographs.
- Carries a white pillow with rings attached.
- If younger than 7 years, carries artificial rings.
- If very young, may sit with his parents during ceremony.
- After the ceremony, carries ring pillow upside down so artificial rings will not show.

# WHO PAYS FOR WHAT

**Bride and/or Bride's Family:**

- Engagement party
- Wedding consultant's fee
- Bridal gown, veil and accessories
- Wedding stationery, calligraphy and postage
- Wedding gift for bridal couple
- Groom's wedding ring
- Gifts for bridesmaids
- Bridesmaids' bouquets
- Pre-wedding parties and bridesmaids' luncheon
- Photography and videography
- Bride's medical exam and blood test
- Wedding guest book and other accessories
- Total cost of the ceremony, including location, flowers, music, rental items and accessories
- Total cost of the reception, including location, flowers, music, rental items, accessories, food, beverages,  cake, decorations, favors, etc.
- Transportation for bridal party to ceremony and reception
- Own attire and travel expenses

## Groom and/or Groom's Family:

- Own travel expenses and attire
- Rehearsal dinner
- Wedding gift for bridal couple
- Bride's wedding ring
- Gifts for groom's attendants
- Medical exam for groom including blood test
- Bride's bouquet and going away corsage
- Mothers' and grandmothers' corsages
- All boutonnieres
- Officiant's fee
- Marriage license
- Honeymoon expenses

## Attendants:

- Own attire except flowers
- Travel expenses
- Bridal shower paid for by maid of honor and bridesmaids
- Bachelor party paid for by best man and ushers

# WEDDING FORMATIONS

The following section illustrates the typical ceremony formations (processional, recessional and altar line up) for both Christian and Jewish weddings, as well as the typical formations for the receiving line, head table, and parents' tables at the reception.

These ceremony formations are included in the *Wedding Party Responsibility Cards,* published by Wedding Solutions Publishing, Inc.   This attractive set of cards makes it very easy for your wedding party to remember their place in these formations.   Give one card to each member of your wedding party... they will appreciate it.

The *Wedding Party Responsibility Cards* are available at most major bookstores or can be ordered directly from the publisher by filling out the Order Form on page 259.

# CHRISTIAN CEREMONY

## ALTAR LINE UP

Bride's Pews          Groom's Pews

### ABBREVIATIONS

| | |
|---|---|
| B = Bride | GF = Groom's Father |
| G = Groom | GM = Groom's Mother |
| BM = Best Man | BMa = Bridesmaids |
| MH = Maid of Honor | U = Ushers |
| BF = Bride's Father | FG = Flower Girl |
| BMo = Bride's Mother | RB = Ring Bearer |
| | O = Officiant |

# CHRISTIAN CEREMONY

PROCESSIONAL          RECESSIONAL

### ABBREVIATIONS

| | |
|---|---|
| B = Bride | GF = Groom's Father |
| G = Groom | GM = Groom's Mother |
| BM = Best Man | BMa = Bridesmaids |
| MH = Maid of Honor | U = Ushers |
| BF = Bride's Father | FG = Flower Girl |
| BMo = Bride's Mother | RB = Ring Bearer |
| | O = Officiant |

# Jewish Ceremony

## Altar Line Up

Groom's Pews                     Bride's Pews

### Abbreviations

| | |
|---|---|
| B = Bride | GF = Groom's Father |
| G = Groom | GM = Groom's Mother |
| BM = Best Man | BMa = Bridesmaids |
| MH = Maid of Honor | U = Ushers |
| BF = Bride's Father | FG = Flower Girl |
| BMo = Bride's Mother | RB = Ring Bearer |
| | R = Rabbi |

# JEWISH CEREMONY

**PROCESSIONAL**          **RECESSIONAL**

## ABBREVIATIONS

| | |
|---|---|
| B = Bride | GF = Groom's Father |
| G = Groom | GM = Groom's Mother |
| BM = Best Man | BMa = Bridesmaids |
| MH = Maid of Honor | U = Ushers |
| BF = Bride's Father | FG = Flower Girl |
| BMo = Bride's Mother | RB = Ring Bearer |
| | R = Rabbi |

## Receiving Line

## Head Table

## Parents' Table

### Abbreviations

| | |
|---|---|
| B = Bride | GF = Groom's Father |
| G = Groom | GM = Groom's Mother |
| BM = Best Man | BMa = Bridesmaids |
| MH = Maid of Honor | U = Ushers |
| BF = Bride's Father | OR = Other Relatives |
| BMo = Bride's Mother | O = Officiant |

# THINGS TO BRING

## TO THE REHEARSAL

### Bride's List:

- ❑ Wedding announcements (for maid of honor to mail after the wedding)
- ❑ Bridesmaids' gifts (if not already given)
- ❑ Camera and film
- ❑ Fake bouquet or ribbon bouquet from bridal shower
- ❑ Groom's gift (if not already given)
- ❑ Reception maps and wedding programs
- ❑ Rehearsal information and ceremony formations
- ❑ Flower girl basket and ring bearer pillow
- ❑ Seating diagrams for head table and parents' tables
- ❑ Wedding schedule of events/timeline
- ❑ Tape player with wedding music

### Groom's List:

- ❑ Bride's gift (if not already given)
- ❑ Marriage license
- ❑ Ushers' gifts (if not already given)
- ❑ Service providers' fees to give to best man or wedding consultant so s/he can pay them at the wedding

## TO THE CEREMONY

### Bride's List:

- ❏ Aspirin/Alka Seltzer
- ❏ Bobby pins
- ❏ Breath spray/mints
- ❏ Bridal gown
- ❏ Bridal gown box
- ❏ Cake knife
- ❏ Change of clothes for going away
- ❏ Clear nail polish
- ❏ Deodorant
- ❏ Garter
- ❏ Gloves
- ❏ Groom's ring
- ❏ Guest book
- ❏ Hair brush
- ❏ Hair spray
- ❏ Head piece
- ❏ Iron
- ❏ Jewelry
- ❏ Kleenex
- ❏ Lint brush
- ❏ Luggage
- ❏ Make-up
- ❏ Mirror
- ❏ Nail polish
- ❏ Panty hose
- ❏ Passport
- ❏ Perfume
- ❏ Personal camera
- ❏ Plume pen for guest book
- ❏ Powder

- ❏ Purse
- ❏ Safety pins
- ❏ Scotch tape/masking tape
- ❏ Sewing kit
- ❏ Shoes
- ❏ Something old
- ❏ Something new
- ❏ Something borrowed
- ❏ Something blue
- ❏ Spot remover
- ❏ Straight pins
- ❏ Tampons or sanitary napkins
- ❏ Toasting goblets
- ❏ Toothbrush & paste

## Groom's List:

- ❏ Airline tickets
- ❏ Announcements
- ❏ Aspirin/Alka Seltzer
- ❏ Breath spray/mints
- ❏ Bride's ring
- ❏ Change of clothes for going away
- ❏ Cologne
- ❏ Cuff Links
- ❏ Cummerbund
- ❏ Deodorant
- ❏ Hair comb
- ❏ Hair spray
- ❏ Kleenex
- ❏ Lint brush
- ❏ Luggage
- ❏ Neck tie
- ❏ Passport

- ❑   Shirt
- ❑   Shoes
- ❑   Socks
- ❑   Toothbrush & paste
- ❑   Tuxedo
- ❑   Underwear

# PAYMENT TRACKING CHART

| Ceremony Site | Contract Date | Total Cost |
|---|---|---|
| Deposit/Date | Next Pay/Date | Final Pay/Date |

| Clergy Services | Contract Date | Total Cost |
|---|---|---|
| Deposit/Date | Next Pay/Date | Final Pay/Date |

| Reception Site | Contract Date | Total Cost |
|---|---|---|
| Deposit/Date | Next Pay/Date | Final Pay/Date |

| Caterer | Contract Date | Total Cost |
|---|---|---|
| Deposit/Date | Next Pay/Date | Final Pay/Date |

# Payment Tracking

# Chart

| Photographer | Contract Date | Total Cost |
|---|---|---|
| Deposit/Date | Next Pay/Date | Final Pay/Date |

| Videographer | Contract Date | Total Cost |
|---|---|---|
| Deposit/Date | Next Pay/Date | Final Pay/Date |

| Music (Cerem.) | Contract Date | Total Cost |
|---|---|---|
| Deposit/Date | Next Pay/Date | Final Pay/Date |

| Music (Recep.) | Contract Date | Total Cost |
|---|---|---|
| Deposit/Date | Next Pay/Date | Final Pay/Date |

# *P*AYMENT *T*RACKING *C*HART

| **Florist** | Contract Date | Total Cost |
|---|---|---|
| Deposit/Date | Next Pay/Date | Final Pay/Date |

| **Bridal Boutique** | Contract Date | Total Cost |
|---|---|---|
| Deposit/Date | Next Pay/Date | Final Pay/Date |

| **Stationary** | Contract Date | Total Cost |
|---|---|---|
| Deposit/Date | Next Pay/Date | Final Pay/Date |

| **Decorations** | Contract Date | Total Cost |
|---|---|---|
| Deposit/Date | Next Pay/Date | Final Pay/Date |

# Payment Tracking Chart

| Limousine | Contract Date | Total Cost |
|---|---|---|
| Deposit/Date | Next Pay/Date | Final Pay/Date |

| Tuxedo Rental | Contract Date | Total Cost |
|---|---|---|
| Deposit/Date | Next Pay/Date | Final Pay/Date |

| Bakery | Contract Date | Total Cost |
|---|---|---|
| Deposit/Date | Next Pay/Date | Final Pay/Date |

| Rental Items | Contract Date | Total Cost |
|---|---|---|
| Deposit/Date | Next Pay/Date | Final Pay/Date |

# Easy Wedding Planning Software

# for Windows

# User's Manual

# *U*ser's *M*anual *C*ontents

# WELCOME TO
# EASY WEDDING PLANNING

Welcome to *Easy Wedding Planning Software for Windows!* This software gives you the ability to completely organize and manage all of your necessary wedding plans. It was designed with two things in mind: first, to enable you to store and quickly retrieve all of the many details pertaining to your wedding (expenses, things to do, guests, etc); and second, to be as easy to use and as intuitive as possible.

Read this User's Manual completely. Even though most of the material will be available via easy access to the program Help File, there are a few items of important information in this manual which will help to get you started. We are confident that you will enjoy planning your wedding with the help of *Easy Wedding Planning Software for Windows*, and we wish you the most beautiful, glorious and memorable wedding ever!

The free version included with this book will allow you to: input wedding information; create guest lists; track service provider information and payment history; record checklists of tasks completed and date due; enter a gift log for all gifts received; and create a complete budget analysis. This program is detailed and easy to use...everything you need to plan your wedding is as simple as clicking a button!

You can upgrade this version to include several other great wedding planning features. See page 238 for details.

# *Getting Started*

Before installing the *Easy Wedding Planning* software, take a few minutes to go over the material in this section and make sure that your computer meets the minimum requirements indicated below.

## TO RUN *EASY WEDDING PLANNING* YOU NEED:

An IBM-compatible personal computer with an 80386sx or 80386 or better processor (an 80386/33MHz or higher is recommended)

A hard disk with 6 megabytes of free space

A Microsoft Mouse or compatible pointing device

An EGA or higher resolution monitor (VGA or higher is recommended)

4 megabytes of RAM

Microsoft Windows version 3.1 or later with MS-DOS version 3.1 or later (version 5.0 or later recommended), Windows 95, or Windows 98

A CD-Rom Drive

# To Set Up
# Easy Wedding Planning

1. Insert CD-Rom in CD-Rom drive.

2. Start Microsoft Windows. If already started we recommend closing all open applications before proceeding.

3. Select the **File** menu in the Windows Program Manager. Then select **Run**.

4. Enter **D** (or **E**):**\SETUP** in the Command Line, depending on the designation of theCD-Rom drive.

5. Choose **OK**.

6. Follow the instructions appearing on the screen:

   a) In the "Welcome" screen, choose (click on) **OK** to begin.

   b) In the "Directory" screen, click on **OK** to select the default directory **C:\WINDOWS\EASYWED**.

Note: If you wish to install the files to a different directory, click on **Change Directory**. You will be presented with a list of directories on your hard disk. Select by double-clicking on the directory of your choice or by  typing in a new or existing directory. Click on **OK**. Then click on **OK** again to confirm your choice.

c) In the "Begin Installation" screen, click on the large button that has a picture of a computer on it.

d) In the "Program Group" screen, click on **OK** to select Easy Wedding Planning for the Program Group to contain the icons, or select a different group from the list shown. You may also enter a new group if you wish. Click on **OK** to complete the installation.

Please note! The *Easy Wedding Planning* software cannot be run from the CD-Rom disk. It must be installed on your hard drive as indicated above and run as indicated in the next chapter.

# *T*O *R*UN
# *E*ASY *W*EDDING *P*LANNING

You run *Easy Wedding Planning* the same way that you run other Windows-based applications. First, open the "Easy Wedding Planning" icon.

There are four items in the *Easy Wedding Planning* program, distinguished by icons having different colored backgrounds.

Ordinarily, you will only need to run the item labeled "Easy Wedding Planning" (red background). This is the actual program.
As you use the program, the data base expands and can become fragmented; that is, 'scattered' over unconnected sectors on your hard disk. When this occurs, pogram operation becomes slower and less efficient.

Also, if you do not exit *Easy Wedding Planning* properly, either by inadvertently shutting down your computer or because of a power failure, the data base may become damaged. In the latter case you will see an error message when you try to open the program, and it will be necessary to repair the data base. You must do this by running (double-clicking on) the item labeled "Repair and Compact" (blue background).

It is probably a good idea to run this item from time to time anyway, especially if the program seems to be slowing down and operating in a sluggish manner. After repairing the data base you will be prompted to begin compacting. Click on **OK** or press the **Enter** key to complete the operation.

The item labeled "Workgroup Administrator" (black background) rarely needs to be run. If the workgroup database file "SYSTEM.MDA" becomes corrupted, you will receive an error message when you try to open the program, prompting you to run this item. Occasionally, this happens during the initial setup. Select **Create** from the Dialog Box which appears.

The item labeled "Read Me First (green background) presents the foregoing text on the screen.

# General Program Information

## THE FORM SCREENS

It is possible to navigate through any form by moving the mouse pointer and clicking or by pressing the **Tab** key on the keyboard. The latter moves to the next field on the form. Holding down the **Shift** key while pressing **Tab** moves back to the previous field. Using the mouse enables you to move to any field to enter data. Data can be entered in either of two ways.

First, by simply typing it in from the keyboard when you see the cursor | or typing it over data already entered. Second, by utilizing data already available in a table. Certain fields have a small arrow button located to their right. Clicking on this arrow button brings up a list of items previously entered in the field, or provided in the program library. Clicking on one of these items causes that item to be entered automatically in the field.

## THE COMMAND BUTTONS

Nearly all operations are controlled by command buttons which appear on every form screen.

The buttons common to most of the screens and the events resulting from clicking them are:

**Help**   brings up a relevant topic or a choice of topics in the Help file

**Report** shows how a printed report will look, along with print option buttons

**Save**   saves all data entered on the screen as a record

**Close**  closes the form and returns to the Control Panel screen

**Delete** deletes the record on screen, as well as all data, and returns to the previous record

The **Guest List** and **Service Providers** screens have three additional buttons:

**Find**   brings up a small subscreen which enables you to search for and retrieve a record

**New**    brings up a blank form for entering new data

**Add**    saves the data on screen as a record and brings up a blank form for new data

Other command buttons also appear and are discussed within the section of the form screen in which they appear.

## THE MENU BAR

All activities within this program can be performed with the mouse, using the keyboard only for entering data. A single-item menu bar is provided at the top of the screen so that a few functions are available in case your mouse malfunctions. The menu bar contains the word **File**. You can activate the menu either by moving the mouse pointer to **File** and clicking, or by holding down the **Alt** key while striking **F** on the keyboard.

When activated by either method, a short menu appears consisting of the entries **Close**, **Save**, and **Exit**. Clicking on any of these entries causes the corresponding action to occur. Alternatively, the desired action can be activated by striking the key indicated by the underlined letter: **C** to close the form, **S** to save all data entered on the form, or **x** to exit the program and return to Windows. Either upper- or lower-case letters may be used.

It is possible to navigate the menus with the up- and down-arrow keys on the keyboard. When the desired action is highlighted, activate it by striking the **Enter** key.

If you do not wish to activate any of the menu actions, click anywhere outside the menu or strike the **Esc** key on the keyboard.

All of these actions are available by clicking on command buttons on the form screen, but the menu provides an alternative should the mouse become disabled or fail to respond.

# &#x1D4AF;HE &#x210B;ELP &#x1D4A3;ILE

The *Easy Wedding Planning* program includes an extensive online Help system, which is accessed by clicking on the **Help** button in any of the forms. The Help system consists of two Help files: one for help in using the program and one which is an online version of *Easy Wedding Planning*. Clicking on the **Help** button brings up a relevant topic or a menu of choices in the Help system.

When a Help topic appears, a row of buttons appears near the top. Clicking on these buttons results in the following actions:

**Contents**  Brings up the Help file Table of Contents

**Search**  Not used

**Back**  Displays the previous Help screen (inactive when Help file is first opened)

**History**  Displays a list of topics examined during the current. Help session. Selecting from this list displays the topic selected.

**Exit Help**  Returns to the form

**Using Help**  Displays this section

It is possible to jump directly to other Help topics by clicking on any word or character appearing in green. Thus you can display the Help topic for any item listed in the Table of Contents by clicking on the topic desired.

Using the top menu bar should not be necessary. For further information about the items on this menu bar, please refer to your Windows documentation.

# The Reports

Each of the forms has an associated report containing the data in printable form. The reports can be viewed by clicking on the command button labeled **Report** on the form in view. There will also appear a menu box containing the option buttons **Print**, **Cancel**, and **Help**. Clicking on the **Print** button invokes the standard Windows printing process. For further information please refer to the Windows User's Guide.

Clicking on the **Cancel** button returns to the form. The mouse pointer is in the form of a magnifying glass. Clicking the mouse displays the entire page as it would appear if printed. Clicking again magnifies the view for closer inspection. You can navigate over the report by using the arrow buttons on the scroll bars or the triangle buttons on the page selector bar at the lower left-hand corner of the screen.

You may also use the **File** menu, indicated by a single-item menu bar at the top of the screen. Either click on **File** or hold down the **Alt** key while striking the **F** key. A short menu will appear with the entries **Close**, **Print**, and **Setup**. The appropriate action will be activated by clicking on the entry desired or by striking the underlined key on the keyboard.

Striking **C** will close the report and return to the form. Striking **P** will activate the standard Windows printing process. Either upper- or lower-case letters may be used. You may also navigate the menus with the up- and down-arrow keys. When the desired action is highlighted, it can be activated by striking the **Enter** key.

# $\mathscr{C}$ONTROL $\mathscr{P}$ANEL

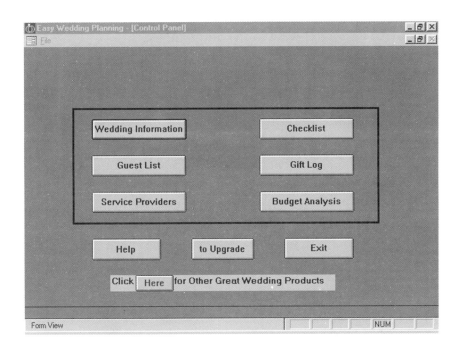

The **Control Panel** consists of six command buttons labeled **Wedding Information, Guest List**, **Service Providers**, **Checklist**, **Gift Log,** and **Budget Analysis**. Moving the mouse pointer to any of these buttons and clicking the left button will bring up the respective screen, which will act as a form for entering data into the data base or as a selection list for additional forms, such as **Checklist** or **Budget Analysis**. If this is the first time you are using this program, you should begin with **Wedding Information**.

Clicking on the **Help** button will bring up a selection menu.

Click on the button next to **EWP Table of Contents** if you need help in planning your wedding. Clicking on any of the items in the Table of Contents will bring up the text associated with that topicClick on the button next to **Using the Control Panel** if you need help in using this program. Click on the button next to **Return to Control Panel** to return to the program.

Clicking on **Exit** will exit the program and return to Windows.

# 𝒲EDDING 𝒥NFORMATION

When this screen appears, the field for the bride's first name will either contain a cursor | or be highlighted (white on black). To move to a different field use the mouse or **Tab** key.

This form screen contains simple text fields only. Simply type in the data. The two **Date** fields will be formatted automatically like 03-Jan-95. The two **Time** fields will be formatted automatically like 10:00 PM. When typing the locations, press the **Enter** key to move to a new line in the field.

# $\mathscr{G}$UEST $\mathscr{L}$IST

| Easy Wedding Planning - [Guest List] | | | _ 🗗 ✕ |
|---|---|---|---|
| File | | | _ 🗗 ✕ |

| | Salutation | First Name | Last Name | |
|---|---|---|---|---|
| First Line: | Mr. | John | Smith | **Inner Envelope** |
| Second Line: | Ms. | Mary | Clarke | |

Address: 145 Fourth Avenue

City: Boston    State: MA    Zip Code: 02345

**Guests in Party**

Telephone: 508-555-3399    Relationship: Friend of Groom

Lodging: Ritz Carlton    Wedding Party:

| Invitations - This Guest | | | Totals - All Guests | | |
|---|---|---|---|---|---|
| **Number of Guests** | Invited | Confirmed | Invited | RSVP | |
| Rehearsal | 0 | 0 | 2 | 1 | **Find** |
| Ceremony | 2 | 0 | 48 | 6 | **New** |
| Reception | 2 | 0 | 48 | 8 | **Add** |
| Announcement | [x] | | 2 | | **Delete** |

| Help | Report | Save | Close | Delete |
|---|---|---|---|---|

| Form View | FLTR | NUM |
|---|---|---|

This form screen enables you to enter the necessary information pertaining to each guest. The fields at the top of the form contain the name(s), title(s), and address information as they should appear on the outer envelope. To record the information for the inner envelope, click on the command button labeled **Inner Envelope**. For help in addressing envelopes, click on the command button labeled **Help** and then click on the button to the right of **Addressing Envelopes** in the dialog box.

Several fields appear with a small arrow button to their right. Clicking on this button brings up a list of items (last names, cities, etc.) entered in previous records or provided with the program. This is a convenient way of entering data without having to retype the same information you entered in a previous record. Simply click on the desired item in the list and it will appear automatically in the field.

Alternatively, you may enter data by typing it in from the keyboard. The program will assist you by inserting an item from the list, matching the first characters you type. You may use this item by moving immediately to another field. If you do not wish to use this item, simply continue to type the data you wish, or press the **Delete** key on the keyboard. If you enter an item not already in the list, it will be added automatically as soon as you move to another field. If you want to delete an item from the list, click on the item and then hold down the **Ctrl** key and strike **Delete** on the keyboard.

The box labeled **Guest Invitation** contains fields for entering the number of guests associated with the person(s) indicated at the top of the Form. It also contains a small box for indicating that an announcement should be sent instead of an invitation.  This is shown by an **x** in the small box. To activate or change this indicator, simply move the mouse pointer to this box and click.

The box labeled **Guest List Totals** contains the totals from all Guest List records. These fields are computed automatically as you enter numbers in the **Guest Invitation** box. Do not attempt to enter data in any of the **Totals** fields directly from the keyboard.

## TO ENTER A NEW GUEST

You may start entering information about a new guest when the screen is completely blank. When you are done, save this information by clicking on the **Save** button. Click on the **Add** button to save and get a new screen for entering the next guest. If you click on the **New** button, you will be prompted to save the information you have entered since the last time you saved data.

## TO FIND AN EXISTING GUEST

To find an existing guest or record, click on the **Find** button. A dialog box will appear with a list of names identifying all existing records. You can view all names by clicking on the arrow buttons on the vertical scroll bar to the right of the list. Make your selection by clicking on the desired name. The form will appear automatically with the information from the desired record. You may then edit or change the data as required.

## TO DELETE AN EXISTING GUEST

If you wish to delete the guest currently shown on the screen, click on the **Delete** button. This will delete the entire record associated with the guest shown at the top of the form. You will then be prompted to confirm that you wish to do so. Click on **Yes** if you do or on **No** if you do not.

To delete any other guest, simply click on the **Find** button to find that guest. Then select the guest you would like to delete. The desired record will then appear on the screen and can be deleted as above.

## TO ADD A NEW GUEST

You can add a new guest in two different ways:
The most common way is to click on the **Add** button. The software will automatically save the information of the record you are working on and give you a new blank form for entering information about the new guest.

If you click on the **New** button, you will be prompted to save the data of the guest presently shown, unless you have already done so. You will have the option to answer **Yes, No,** or **Cancel** by clicking on the appropriate button. Clicking on **Cancel** will return you to the record on which you were working; otherwise a new blank form will appear.

## TO UPDATE OR CHANGE INFORMATION ON AN EXISTING GUEST

To change information about a guest currently on the screen, simply place the cursor on the field where you want to enter or change information. You can use the **Tab** key or the mouse. Once the cursor is in that field, simply enter the information you wish. If there is already some information you would like to delete, use the delete key on your keyboard or highlight the information to be deleted by dragging your mouse (holding down the left button) over the data and then striking the **Delete** key. To save the data in a record, click on the **Save** button.

## TO PRINT A REPORT

When you wish to view or print a report of guest list data, click on the **Report** button. You will have three choices from the print menu: **Names and Addresses, Complete Records,** or **Cancel.** If you select (click on) either of the first two options, the screen will show the report as it will be printed and give you the choice to print or cancel. If you select **Print** the software will provide the standard Windows printing procedure.

If you do not wish to print the report at this time, simply click on the **Cancel** button and you will return directly to the form.

# SERVICE PROVIDERS

| Easy Wedding Planning - [Service Providers] |
|---|

File

| | | | |
|---|---|---|---|
| **Company** | Flowers by Stephanie | **Contact** | Stephanie Rogers |
| **Address** | 123 First Avenue | **Service** | Flowers |
| **City** | San Diego | **State** | CA | **Zip** | 92011 |
| **Telephone** | 619-589-4985 | | |
| **Cost** | $3,500.00 | **Contract Date** | 01-Jan-00 | **Paid by** | Bride's Family |

|  | Due Date | Amount | Paid | Notes |
|---|---|---|---|---|
| **Payment 1** | 01-Sep-00 | $500.00 | ☒ | check #798 |
| **Payment 2** | 01-Jun-00 | $1,500.00 | ☐ | will call to review samples |
| **Payment 3** | 01-Sep-01 | $1,500.00 | ☐ | due wedding day |
| **Payment 4** | | $0.00 | ☐ | |
| **Remaining Balance** | | $3,000.00 | | |

Find   New   Add

Help   Report   Save   Close   Delete

Form View                                     NUM

This form screen enables you to record all necessary information regarding the expenses to be incurred in conjunction with the wedding. In this screen you will enter all necessary information pertaining to each purchase or service provider; i. e. ceremony site, reception site, photographer, videographer, florist, etc. The name of the company providing the service is entered at the top of the form in the first field. Other fields at the top of the form screen are for entering data such as the name of the person to contact, address, telephone number, type of service to be provided, etc.

Several fields appear with a small arrow button to their right. Clicking on this button brings up a list of items (cities, etc.) entered in previous records, and in some cases (wedding party, paid by) provided with the program. This is a convenient way of entering data without having to retype data you entered in a previous record. Simply click on the desired item from the list and it will appear automatically in that field.

Alternatively, you may enter data by typing it in from the keyboard. The program will attempt to assist you by inserting an item from the list, matching the first character(s) you type in one of these fields. You may use this item by moving immediately to another field. If you do not wish to use this item, you may simply continue to type the data you wish or press the **Delete** key on the keyboard. If you enter an item not already in the list it will be added to the list automatically as soon as you move to another field. If you want to delete an item from the list, click on the item and then hold down the **Ctrl** key while striking the **Delete** key on the keyboard.

For help in determining expense allocation, click on the command button labeled **Help** and then click on the button to the right of **Who Pays for What** in the dialog box. This will bring up the section of the Help file giving suggestions as to who might be expected to pay for what. The bottom half of the form contains fields for entering the payment information for the particular service indicated. The remaining balance is calculated automatically.

## TO ENTER A PURCHASE OR SERVICE PROVIDER

If the screen is completely blank, you may start entering information about a particular purchase or service provider. When you are done, save the information by clicking on the **Save** button. Click on the **Add** button to save it and get a new screen for entering the next purchase or service provider. If you click on the

**New** button, you will be prompted to save the information you have entered since the last time you saved the data.

## TO FIND AN EXISTING PURCHASE OR SERVICE PROVIDER

To find an existing service provider or record, click on the **Find** button. A dialog box will appear with an alphabetical list of purchases or service providers identifying all existing records. You can view all purchases or service providers by clicking the arrow buttons on the vertical scroll bar to the right of the list. Make your selection by clicking on the desired purchase or service provider. The form will appear automatically with the information from the desired record. You may then edit, change or delete data as required.

## TO DELETE AN EXISTING PURCHASE OR SERVICE PROVIDER

To delete the purchase or service provider currently shown on the screen, click on the **Delete** button. This will delete the entire record associated with that purchase. You will be prompted to confirm that you wish to do so. Click on **Yes** if you do or on **No** if you do not.

To delete any other purchase or service provider, click on the **Find** button to find that purchase or service provider. Then select the record you would like to delete. The record will appear on the screen and can be deleted asexplained above.

## TO ADD A NEW PURCHASE OR SERVICE PROVIDER

You can add a new purchase or service provider in two different ways:

The most common way to add a new purchase or service provider is to click on the **Add** button. The software will automatically save the information of the record you are working on and give you a new blank form in which to enter information about the new purchase or service provider.

If you click on the **New** button, you will be prompted to save the data of the purchase or service provider shown unless you have already done so. You will have the option of answering **Yes, No,** or **Cancel** by clicking on the appropriate button. Clicking on **Cancel** will return you to the record on which you are working; otherwise a new blank form will appear.

## TO UPDATE/CHANGE INFORMATION ON AN EXISTING PURCHASE OR SERVICE PROVIDER

To change information about the purchase or service provider currently on the screen, simply place the cursor on the field where you want to enter or change information. You can use the **Tab** key or the mouse. Once the cursor is in that field, simply enter the information you wish. If there is already some information that you want to delete, use the **Delete** key on your keyboard or highlight the information to be deleted by dragging your mouse (holding down the left button) over the data and then striking the **Delete** key.

To save the data in a record, click on the **Save** button.

## TO PRINT A REPORT

When you wish to view or print a report of the purchase or service provider data, click on the **Report** button. You will have three choices: **This Record Only, All Records**, or **Cancel**. If you select (click on) either of the first two options, the screen will show the report as it will be printed and give you the choice to print or cancel. If you select **Print,** the software will provide the standard Windows printing procedures.

To close the form screen, click on the **Close** button and you will return to the main **Control Panel**.

# 𝓒HECKLISTS

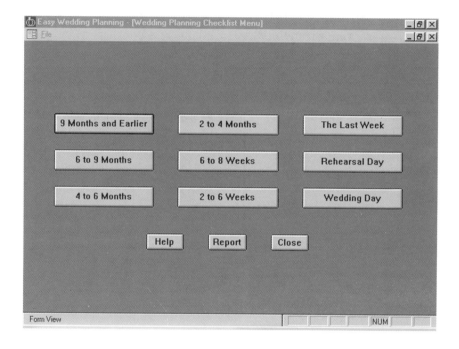

This screen controls access to the records of tasks which should be accomplished within certain time intervals prior to the wedding. The nine large command buttons in the center of the screen are labeled with various time intervals during which certain tasks should be taken care of. Clicking on any of these buttons brings up the form containing the records associated with the corresponding time interval.

Clicking on the button labeled **Report** brings up a choice of nine time intervals, or **Print All**. Clicking on the selected time interval button will bring up the report containing that list of tasks. You can view or print the report by clicking on the appropriate button in the superimposed box. Clicking on **Print All** will result in printing all nine reports. Clicking on the **Close** button will return you to the **Control Panel**.

The forms containing the task lists show the records in table format. The lists of **Tasks** are taken from the book *Easy Wedding Planner*. You are free to edit, add to, or delete from this list as desired and appropriate in your case. Enter the name of the individual who is responsible for a particular task in the **Who** field. These fields have an arrow button to their right. Clicking on this button brings up a list of roles supplied by the program. Simply click on the desired item in the list and it will appear automatically in the field.

Alternatively, you may enter data by typing it in from the keyboard, and your entry will be added to the list. The small boxes arranged in a vertical column under **Done** are either blank or have the indicator **x**, indicating that the task has been completed. To change this indicator, simply move the mouse pointer to the appropriate box and click.

The **Date** fields are calculated from the wedding date entered on the **Wedding Information** form. If the task is done, the **Days Left** field will indicate 0. If the due date is past, the number in the **Days Left** field will appear in red.

The data you enter is saved automatically when you move to a new record, close the form, or change to a different time interval. You can change time intervals by clicking the arrow button on the **Stage** field at the top of the screen. If you wish to delete a record, click on the **Delete** button. This will delete the entire record indicated by the record selector. You will be prompted to confirm that you wish to do so.

Click on **Yes** if you do or on **No** if you do not. When you wish to view or print a report of your tasks, click on the **Report** button. You may then view the report or print it by clicking the corresponding button in the dialog box. To close the form screen, click on **Close.** This will return you to the **Checklist** control screen.

# $\mathscr{G}$IFT $\mathscr{L}$OG

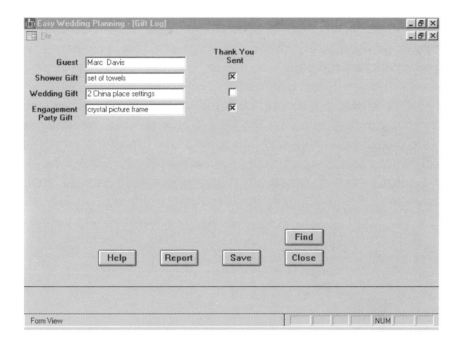

The **Gift Log** allows you to enter information about gifts received from individuals on your **Guest List**. Fields are provided for the entry of gift data from the individuals listed on the first and second lines of the **Guest List** form. This form is controlled by the **Find** button. Clicking on this button will bring up a list of recorded guests, both first and second line names. You can move back and forth from the first line name and the second line name by clicking on the arrow buttons on the horizontal scroll bar. You can view the names of all recorded guests by clicking on the arrow buttons on the vertical scroll bar. Make your selection by clicking on the name(s) of the desired guest.

The gift information pertaining to that guest (or those guests in a two-name record) will then appear on the screen for editing or may be entered in the blank fields. Do not enter data from the keyboard into the fields labeled **Guest**. The small boxes arranged in a vertical column under **Thank You Sent** are either blank or have the indicator **x**, indicating that a thank-you note has been sent. To change this indicator, simply move the mouse pointer to the appropriate box and click.

To save the data in a record, click on the **Save** button. If you wish to delete a record, click on the **Delete** button. This will delete the entire record associated with the name at the top of the form. You will be prompted to confirm that you wish to do so. Click on **Yes** if you do or on **No** if you do not. When you wish to view or print a report of Gift Log data, click on the **Report** button. You may then view the report or print it by clicking  the corresponding button in the dialog box. To close the form screen, click on the **Close** button and you will return to the main **Control Panel**.

# BUDGET ANALYSIS

| Easy Wedding Planning - [Budget Analysis] | | | | | | _ 🗗 ✕ |
|---|---|---|---|---|---|---|
| File | | | | | | _ 🗗 ✕ |

| Budget Total: | | $15,000.00 | | Tax Rate: | 7.75% | |
|---|---|---|---|---|---|---|
| **Category** | **Typical** | **Budgeted** | **Category** | **Typical** | **Budgeted** | |
| Ceremony | $900.00 | $950.00 | Bakery | $300.00 | $269.64 | |
| Wedding Attire | $1,500.00 | $1,202.75 | Flowers | $900.00 | $3,661.63 | |
| Photography | $1,350.00 | $1,643.19 | Transportation | $300.00 | $323.25 | |
| Videography | $750.00 | $592.63 | Gifts | $450.00 | $404.06 | |
| Stationery | $600.00 | $700.38 | Parties | $600.00 | $592.63 | |
| Reception | $6,000.00 | $7,542.50 | Miscellaneous | $600.00 | $16.16 | |
| Music | $750.00 | $538.75 | | | | |
| | | | | Total | $18,437.56 | |

| Help | Report | Close |
|---|---|---|

Form View          NUM

There are only two fields in which you should enter data in this form screen. Enter the total amount of money available to be spent in the first field, **Budget Total**. Enter the local sales tax rate in % in the **Tax Rate** field.

There are 13 Budget Categories listed in two columns. The amounts in the **Typical** columns are percentages of the Budget Total based on suggestions in *Easy Wedding Planning* and are intended to be a guide. The amounts in the **Budgeted** column are calculated automatically as the sum of all budget items within the individual categories. To access these budget items, click on the appropriate category button (e. g. **Photography**). The form screen for detailed accounting within the category chosen will appear. To save any new entries, click on the **Save** button. To close the form and return to the **Control Panel**, click on the **Close** button.

Clicking on the **Report** button will bring up a form screen from which you may select a particular Budget Category report to view or print. Simply click on the appropriate button. The **Summary** report provides the totals for each of the 13 categories. Clicking on **All** results in printing all 14 reports, including the summary.

The forms for detailed accounting within the individual categories show the records in table format. The lists of items are taken from the book *Easy Wedding Planner*. You are free to edit, add to, or delete from this list as desired and appropriate in your case. Enter the quantity and cost per unit in the next two fields.

The **Cost** field is computed automatically as the product of the **Qty** (quantity) and **Unit Cost** fields for each item. If the item is taxable, click on the small box to the right to show the indicator **x**. The **Subtotal**, **Total Tax**, and **Total** fields are calculated automatically. The amount in the **Total** field is transferred to the main Budget Analysis form when you close the form or change to a different category. You can change categories by clicking the arrow button on the appropriate **Category** field at the top of the form.

The data you enter is saved automatically when you move to a new record, close the form, or change categories. If you wish to delete a record, click on the **Delete** button. This will delete the entire record associated with the selected item. You will be prompted to confirm that you wish to do so. Click on **Yes** if you do or on **No** if you do not. When you wish to view or print a budget report for the category, click on the **Report** button. You may then view the report or print it by clicking the corresponding button in the dialog box. To close the form screen, click on the **Close** button which will return you to the main **Budget Analysis** form.

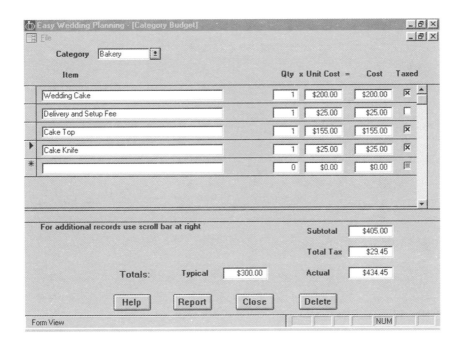

Upon bringing up one of these forms, the selected category appears in the field at the upper right of the form with a small arrow button to its right. Clicking on this button brings up a list of all 13 categories. You may bring up the form for any of these categories at any time by clicking on the category desired. All appropriate data will appear automatically.

The form for the Reception category is a bit more complicated than the rest. Reception expenses are a significant fraction of the total wedding budget and are extremely sensitive to the number of guests anticipated. Therefore some additional fields are included. These fields are labeled **Est No Guests** and **Define Quantity**.

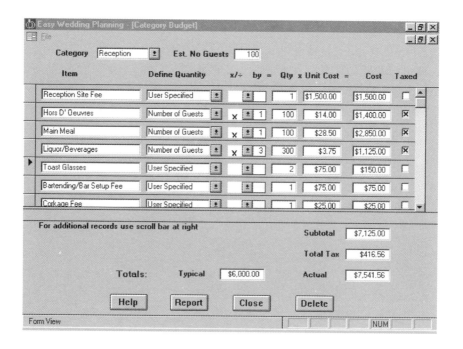

You should enter an estimated number of guests in the field provided. In the latter field, clicking on the arrow button to the right brings up a list of two expressions: **Nmber of Guests** and **User Specified**. The latter is the default entry. Two additional fields are also present and are used if Number of Guests is selected. A division or multiplication sign may be selected by clicking on the next arrow button, depending on whether the quantity is a fraction (e.g. tables) or a multiple (e.g. drinks) of the number of guests. Enter the appropriate factor in the field to the right. The **Qty** field will then be calculated as the number of guests divided or multiplied by the factor you have just entered, and the **Cost** field will be calculated accordingly.

The default entries **x** (under the multiplication/division column) and **1** (under the **Qty** column) indicate that the quantity needed is simply equal to the number of guests. These two fields have no effect on any record in which the **Define Quantity** field is not the number of guests. You can determine the effect of changing the estimated number of guests on the total cost of the reception by entering a new estimated number of guests. All necessary calculations will then be made so you can see the result, and the new data will be saved automatically.

On the other hand, you may ignore the additional fields included with this category and enter the value for the quantity **Qty** directly, just as with the forms for the other categories.

# *T*O *U*PGRADE *E*ASY *W*EDDING *P*LANNING *S*OFTWARE

The free software enclosed in this book offers a basic wedding planning system. With this software, you can use the Help File, The Reports, Control Panel, Wedding Information, Guest List, Service Providers, Checklists, Gift Log, and Budget Analysis. You can upgrade this free version to include features such as: Seating Arrangements for both the ceremony and reception; printing Labels, Envelopes, and Postcards; Wedding Day Schedules and timelines for your wedding party and service providers; and a Stationary Checklist.

You can upgrade this free version to include all of these great features for only $19.95. Simply call Wedding Solutions Publishing, Inc. at (619) 582-1878 to request a passcode that will allow you to upgrade this software.

To obtain this code, call (619) 582-1878 to pay by credit card, or send a check or money order for $19.95 to Wedding Solutions Pubishing, Inc., 6347 Caminito Tenedor, San Diego, CA 92120 (refer to order form on page 259).

After you have installed the upgraded version, your control panel will appear as shown below.

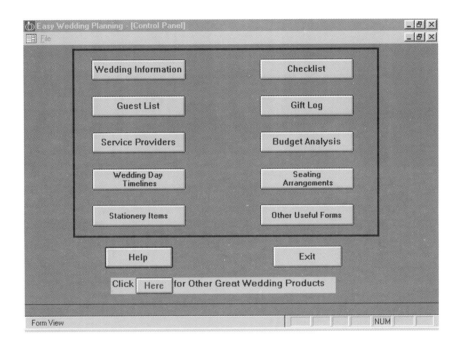

The following manual pages will provide information and support pertaining to these new options.

# SEATING ARRANGEMENTS

The screens for planning the seating arrangements for the Ceremony (pews) and for the Reception (tables) are virtually identical. There are three main panels: **Party to be assigned**, **Party**, and **Pew**. The left panel contains a list of all the guests entered on the first line of the **Guest List** screen. Scrolling to the desired guest and clicking on the name will bring up the names of all the guests in the party of that guest in the middle panel, also showing the pew or table to which he or she has already been assigned. If no assignment has been made, the field will remain blank. To assign (or reassign) a guest to the pew or table indicated in the right panel, double-click on the name of that guest in the middle panel.

You may select the pew or table by entering the number in the space to the right of **Pew** or by selecting the number from the list viewed by clicking the adjacent small arrow button. To assist in planning the seating arrangements, you should enter a number in the space to the right of **Max** to indicate the maximum number of places in the pews or tables. You will be prompted if you exceed this number for any pew or table.

To delete an assigned guest from a pew or table, click on the guest's name in the right panel and then click on the **Delete** button below. When you are finished save your data by clicking on the **Save** button. Clicking on the **Close** button closes the screen and returns you to the **Control Panel**.

Clicking on the **Report** button will allow you to preview the entire seating arrangement and print a copy of it. This button can be activated by obtaining an Upgrade PassCode from Wedding Solutions Publishing, Inc. at (619) 582-1878.

# LABELS

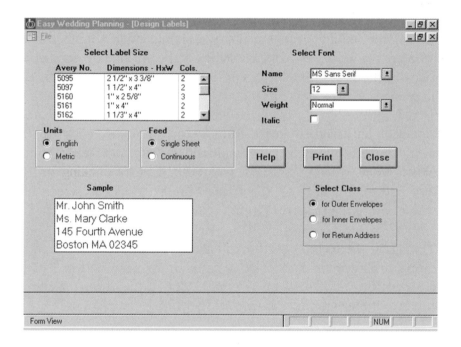

This screen enables you to design and print mailing labels for the guests on your guest list. The panel in the upper left of the screen contains a list of many label sizes available commercially. The panel will list sizes in English or Metric units, and Single Sheet or Continuous feed style. You may design your labels by selecting the font, size, weight, and lettering style. Make your selections by clicking on the small buttons to the right of the space indicated, and clicking on the font or other item desired. If your computer and printer will support a desired font other than those listed, you may enter that font name in the space provided in place of the listed font. After you properly select each font, the **Sample** box at the lower left will display the label appearance.

Clicking on the **Preview** button will allow you to preview the label sheet as it will print, and to print the labels. This function can be activated by obtaining an Upgrade PassCode from Wedding Solutions Publishing, Inc. at (619) 582-1878. Caution: it is best to print the first sheet on a regular sheet of paper to make sure that the information will appear in the correct location of the page. The program is set for normal margin settings as indicated in the Windows Print Manager. Some Windows setups vary.

Clicking on the **Close** button will close the screen and return you to the **Control Panel**.

# 𝓔NVELOPES

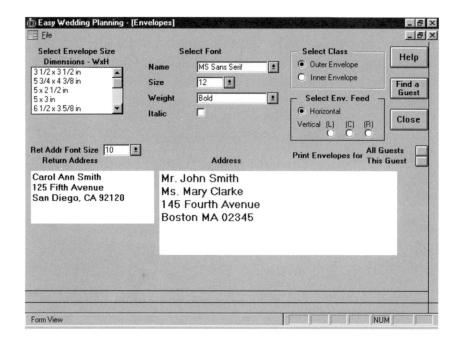

This screen enables you to design and print your invitation envelopes for mailing to the guests on your guest list. The screens for inner and outer envelopes work almost identically. The panel in the upper left of the screen contains a list of various sizes of envelopes available commercially. Select the size which most nearly matches the size of the envelopes you plan to use. Alternatively, you may specify the size of the envelope by scrolling down to the last item in the list to the word "User". Click on this word and you will have the option of entering the envelope size. Enter the envelope width and height in inches and decimal. For instance if the width is 6 3/8 inches, enter **6.375** in the space provided.

Select Outer or Inner Envelope by clicking on the Option Button at the top of the screen under the **Class** menu. The screen for outer envelopes provides a place for entering a return address. You can later change this by clicking on it and editing it. You may select the font, the size, the weight, and whether to italicize the lettering. The font size for the return address may be selected different than that of the main address. Make your selections by clicking on the small buttons to the right of the spaces indicated, and clicking on the font or other item desired. If your computer and printer will support a desired font other than those listed, you may enter that font name in the space provided in place of the listed font. After you properly select each font, the display will change to reflect your selections.

Clicking on the **Find a Guest** button will display a list of all of your primary guests. Find the guest in the database by using the scroll bar, then click on the name of the guest. The display will then show the name and address of the selected guest.

Before printing the envelopes, be sure that you have selected the correct **Feed** for your printer. You may select Horizontal or Vertical for the feed mode by clicking on the Option Button from the **Feed** menu below the **Class** menu. Selecting the Vertical mode will cause the printer to print in landscape mode, with the envelope fed into the bin lengthwise. In Vertical mode you need to select the feed for your particular printer to determine whether the envelope feeds from the right (R), center (C), or left (L) side of the bin. For certain printers, it may be necessary to also select Vertical Feed Adjust, in order to account for the way the printer driver is designed. We suggest that you test this function by printing on scrap paper initially to verify that your settings are correct. Be sure to read your printer manual to properly feed envelopes.

Clicking on the button **Print Envelope for** will allow you to preview the envelopes as they will be printed, and to print the envelopes. You can do this for all guests in your guest list or for only the guest shown on the graphic display envelope by clicking on the button indicated. This function can be activated by obtaining an Upgrade PassCode from Wedding Solutions Publishing, Inc. at (619) 582-1878.

CAUTION: It may be wise to print the first page (i.e. the first envelope) on a regular sheet of paper to make sure that the addresses will appear in the correct locations.

Clicking on the **Close** button will close the screen and return you to the **Control Panel**.

# 𝒫OSTCARDS

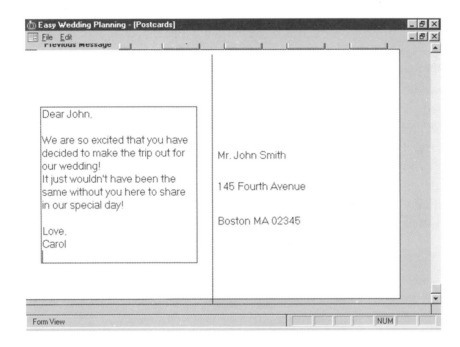

This screen enables you to print postcards. You may select the desired guest from the List Box at the upper left of the screen. The name(s), address, and prior message sent (if any) will appear below in the postcard graphic. Type in or edit the message. If you have just saved a message or printed a postcard for another guest, you may retrieve the previous message by clicking on the button indicated by **Previous Message**. You may select the font, size, weight, and style of the lettering. Make your selections by clicking on the small buttons to the right of the spaces indicated, and clicking on the font or other item desired. If your computer and printer will support a desired font other than those listed, you may enter that font name in the space provided in place of the listed font. After you properly select each font, the display will change to reflect your selections.

Before printing the postcard, be sure that you have selected the correct **Feed** for your printer. You may select Horizontal or Vertical for the feed mode by clicking on the designated Option Button near the top right of the screen. Selecting the Vertical mode will cause the printer to print in landscape mode, with the postcard fed into the bin lengthwise. In Vertical mode you need to select the feed of your particular printer to determine whether the envelopes feed from the right (R), center (C), or left (L) side of the bin. For certain printers, it may be necessary to select Vertical Feed Adjust in order to account for the way the printer driver is designed. We suggest that you test this function by printing on scrap paper initially to verify that your settings are correct. Be sure to read the manual for your printer for properly feeding postcards.

Clicking on the **Print** button allows you to preview the postcard as it will be printed, and to print the postcard. This function can be activated by obtaining an Upgrade PassCode from Wedding Solutions Publishing, Inc. at (619) 582-1878.

CAUTION: It may be wise to print the postcard on a regular sheet of paper to make sure that the name, address, and message will appear in the correct locations.

Clicking on the **Save** button will save the message for the selected guest. Clicking on the **Close** button will close the screen and return you to the **Control Panel**.

# *W*EDDING *D*AY *S*CHEDULES

*Easy Wedding Planning - [Timeline]*
*File*

### *W*EDDING   *P*ARTY   *T*IMELINE

| Time | Event | Bride | Bride's Mother | Bride's Father | Maid of Honor | Bride's Family | Bridesmaids | Groom | Groom's Mother | Groom's Father | Groom's Family | Best Man | Ushers | Flower Girl | Ring Bearer |
|---|---|---|---|---|---|---|---|---|---|---|---|---|---|---|---|
| 10:00 AM | Manicurist Appointment | x | x |  | x | x |  |  |  |  |  |  |  |  |  |
| 10:30 AM | Hair/Makeup Appointment | x | x |  | x | x |  |  |  |  |  |  |  |  |  |
| 12:15 PM | Arrive at Dressing Site | x | x |  | x | x |  |  |  |  |  |  |  |  |  |
| 12:30 PM | Arrive at Dressing Site |  |  |  |  |  |  | x |  |  |  |  |  |  |  |
| 12:45 PM | Pre-Ceremony Photos |  |  |  |  |  |  | x | x | x | x | x | x |  |  |
| 1:15 PM | Arrive at Ceremony Site |  |  |  |  |  |  | x | x | x | x | x | x |  |  |
| 1:15 PM | Pre-Ceremony Photos | x | x | x | x | x | x |  |  |  |  |  |  |  |  |
| 1:20 PM | Give Officiant License and Fee |  |  |  |  |  |  |  |  |  |  | x |  |  |  |
| 1:20 PM | Ushers receive Seating Chart |  |  |  |  |  |  |  |  |  |  |  | x |  |  |
| 1:30 PM | Ushers give Program to Guests |  |  |  |  |  |  |  |  |  |  |  | x |  |  |
| 1:30 PM | Arrive at Ceremony Site |  |  |  |  |  |  |  |  |  |  |  |  | x | x |
| 1:30 PM | Guests sign Guest Book |  |  |  |  |  |  |  |  |  |  |  |  |  |  |
| 1:30 PM | Prelude Music begins |  |  |  |  |  |  |  |  |  |  |  |  |  |  |
| 1:35 PM | Begin seating Guests |  |  |  |  |  |  |  |  |  |  |  | x |  |  |
| 1:45 PM | Arrive at Ceremony Site | x | x | x | x | x | x |  |  |  |  |  |  |  |  |
| 1:45 PM | Honored Guests seated |  |  |  |  |  |  |  |  |  |  |  | x |  |  |
| 1:50 PM | Groom's Parents seated |  |  |  |  |  |  |  | x | x |  |  | x |  |  |
| 1:55 PM | Bride's Mother seated |  | x |  |  |  |  |  |  |  |  |  |  |  |  |

| Help | Print | Sort | Add | Delete | Close |

Form View   NUM

Screens have also been provided to help you plan your busy schedule for the day of your wedding. The screens pertain to the members of the wedding party and to the service providers. They are both centered around the time of the wedding: the event designated "Ceremony begins". The time of this event has been taken from the **Wedding Information** screen. Neither the time nor any other information on this line should be changed on this screen. The other times and events shown are based on the experience of the authors of the book *Easy Wedding Planner*. However they can

can be changed and edited to reflect your personal judgment.  To change the time of any event simply click on the time to be changed and enter the time desired.  You may change the designation of the event in the same way.  To change the applicability to any of the participants listed along the top, simply click in the appropriate box under the participant and on the line of the event.

You may wish to add an event not designated or delete an unnecessary event.  To delete an event simply click on the event to be deleted and click on the **Delete** button at the bottom of the screen.  If you wish to add an event, click on the **Add** button at the bottom of the screen.  A blank line will appear for you to enter the information for this event.  When you are finished click on the **Sort** button and the event you added will appear in the proper location on the screen.   Incidentally, you should perform the sorting whenever you change the time order of the listed events.

Clicking on the **Preview** button will allow you to preview the form as it will be printed, and to print it.  This function can be activated by obtaining an Upgrade PassCode from Wedding Solutions Publishing, Inc. at (619) 582-1878.   Be sure to read your printer manual to properly feed envelopes.

Clicking on the **Close** button will close the screen and return you to the **Control Panel**.

# STATIONERY CHECKLIST

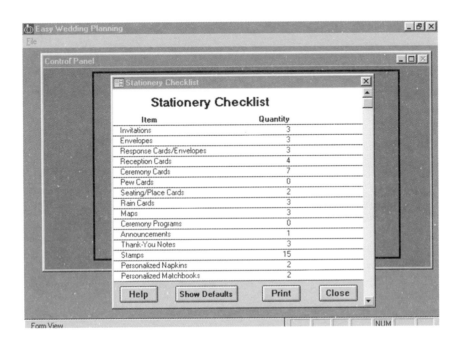

This screen is a list of all of the stationery items associated with your wedding, along with the number required of each of the items. The names of the items should not be edited unless you wish to add a new item or delete an item from any future record. You may enter your estimate for the number of each of the items listed. You can change any of these quantities by clicking on it and entering a new number. Clicking on the **Show Defaults** button will show the **Default** number of each of the items as suggested by the software, and is based on the number of guests who have received announcements, or the number of individuals invited to the Reception and/or the Ceremony.

You can add a new **Item** by going to the empty line at the end of the list and entering the data. If this line is not visible, click on the down-arrow at the lower right corner to begin scrolling until the empty line comes into view. There will be no **Default** number for this item.

Clicking on the **Print** button will allow you to print the **Item** and **Quantity** information. The **Default** values will not appear on the printout. Clicking on the **Close** button will close the screen and return you to the **Control Panel**.

# *D*ATA *B*ACK-*U*P

## BACK UP YOUR DATA!

You should always back up your work. Hard disks do crash, and important files can be accidentally deleted on computers.

In order to back up your *Easy Wedding Planning* data, first insert a formatted 3½-in 1.44-MB floppy disk in your disk drive. There are two ways to proceed. In DOS, go to the directory **C:\WINDOWS\EASYWED**, or the directory where you installed the software, and enter the command **COPY WEDINFO.MDB A:** or **B:**, depending on the designation of your drive. Your floppy disk will then contain your data. If your floppy disk contained an earlier backup of **WEDINFO.MDB**, you may use the DOS **REPLACE** command instead.

In Windows, open the "Main" group in Program Manager. Then open (double-click on) the "File Manager" icon. In the left-hand panel of the window click on **WINDOWS\EASYWED** or the directory where you installed the software from the directory list.

You may need to first click on the icon identifying the correct hard disk partition. The latter choices are arrayed across the top of the window. Then click on **WEDINFO.MDB** in the right-hand panel. Next select **Copy** from the **File** menu, from the menu bar along the top of the window. Enter **A:** or **B:** in the **To** field in the input box which appears. Your floppy disk will then contain a backup copy of your data.

If a disaster occurs, you may need to reinstall the software. Do so from the original set of three disks. Next insert the floppy disk containing the backup copy of **WEDINFO.MDB** in your disk drive. Then, from DOS, either **COPY** or **REPLACE** the file **WEDINFO.MDB** from **A:** or **B:** to the directory where you installed the software.

From Windows, open File Manager as above. Then click on the icon identifying your disk drive (either **A** or **B**). Then click on the entry **WEDINFO.MDB** in the right-hand panel of the window. Next select **Copy** from the **File** menu. Enter the name of the directory where you reinstalled the software, including the drive partition identifier, e.g. **C:\WINDOWS\EASYWED**. You can now resume planning your wedding!

# Wedding Solutions Publishing

proudly presents...

## YOUR BRIDAL SUPERSTORE

...e v e r y t h i n g   b u t   t h e   g r o o m ™

*www.yourbridalsuperstore.com*

...a complete collection of the most beautiful and elegant invitations, accessories and jewelry available.

Low prices, beautiful selection and great quality
make it easy and convenient for you to order
all your wedding accessories from this one location!

See the Wedding Checklist on the following pages for a list of some of the items currently available.

# ~ Wedding Checklist ~

## Wedding Stationery ~

- Invitations
- Announcements
- Reception Enclosures
- Response Card / Envs.
- Map Cards
- At Home Cards

- Bows and Ribbons
- Gift Bags and Wrap
- Thank You Notes
- Calligraphy Pens
- Informals

- Programs
- Photo Seals
- Bookmarks
- Decorative Seals
- Lined Inner Envs.
- Printed Envelopes

## Wedding Party Gifts ~

- Keepsake Box
- Jewelry Heart Box
- Rich Vanilla Candle
- Cigar Trimmer & Case

- Personalized Glassware
- Personalized Flask
- Flower Girl T-shirt, Cap, and stuffed Bear
- Ring Bearer T-shirt, Cap, and stuffed Bear

## Ceremony Essentials ~

- Aisle Runner
- Pew Bows
- Unity Candle

- Guest Book
- Plume Pen
- Gratuity Envelopes
- Flower Girl Basket

- Ring Bearer Pillow or Chest
- Bridal Handbag
- Garters

## Reception Essentials ~

- Cake Knife & Server
- Tissue Bells
- Paper Streamers
- Candy Hearts
- Cake Boxes or Bags
- Book or Box Matches
- Favor Making Supplies
- Balloons
- Place Cards
- Cake Tops
- Cake Top Domes

- Thank You Ribbons & Scrolls
- Thank You Bookmarks
- Wishing Well Card Holder
- Toasting Glasses/Goblets
- Sequined Heart or Chiffon Tie-Ons
- Biodegradable Heart-Shaped Rice
- Wedding Bubbles

- Bouquet Holders
- Cookie Cutter Favors
- Favor Ribbons
- Floating Candles & Glass Cylinder
- Favor Bells
- Memory Albums
- Candy Bar Wrapper Favors
- Glass Candle Favors
- Seeds of Love
- "Just Married" Banner

## Special Items ~

- Gratuity Envelopes
- Parents' Gifts
- Thank You Guide

- Personalized License Plate
- Car Decorating Kit
- Bridal Gown Cover

- Memories Box
- Marriage Certificate
- Wedding Time Capsule

Find these items and many more at:

# www.yourbridalsuperstore.com